THE
FIELD & STREAM

Wilderness
Survival
Handbook

The Field & Stream Library

The Field & Stream *Bowhunting Handbook* by Bob Robb
The Field & Stream *Deer Hunting Handbook*
   by Jerome B. Robinson
The Field & Stream *Firearms Safety Handbook* by Doug Painter
The Field & Stream *Shooting Sports Handbook*
   by Thomas McIntyre
The Field & Stream *Sporting Vehicles Handbook*
   by Slaton L. White
The Field & Stream *Turkey Hunting Handbook*
   by Philip Bourjaily
The Field & Stream *Upland Game Handbook* by Bill Tarrant

The Field & Stream *Baits and Rigs Handbook*
   by C. Boyd Pfeiffer
The Field & Stream *Bass Fishing Handbook* by Mark Sosin and
   Bill Dance
The Field & Stream *Fishing Knots Handbook* by Peter Owen
The Field & Stream *Fish Finding Handbook* by
   Leonard M. Wright Jr.
The Field & Stream *Fly Fishing Handbook*
   by Leonard M. Wright Jr.
The Field & Stream *Tackle Care and Repair Handbook*
   by C. Boyd Pfeiffer
The Field & Stream *Wilderness Cooking Handbook*
   by J. Wayne Fears

THE
FIELD & STREAM
Wilderness Survival Handbook

Len McDougall

THE LYONS PRESS

Guilford, Connecticut
An imprint of The Globe Pequot Press

Printed in Canada

10 9 8 7 6 5 4 3 2 1

The Library of Congress Cataloging-in-Publication Data

McDougall, Len.
     The Field & Stream wilderness survival handbook/Len McDougall.
          p. cm.
     Includes index.
     ISBN 1-55821-228-0
     1.Wilderness survival—Handbooks, manuals, etc. I. Outward Bound, Inc. II. Title.
     GV200.5 .M374 2001
     613.6'9—dc21   00-66004

Contents

Preface

This is a survival book by a man who enjoys the process, a book put together for readers who usually try hard to avoid the whole idea.

We sportsmen rarely set out to survive. But because we are exposed to the wilds more than golfers or tennis fanatics or model airplane racers, we should know what to do if suddenly we find ourselves temporarily disoriented . . . for a day or two.

The very best way to cope with that situation is to avoid it. And the way to avoid it is to learn how to use a map and compass. GPS can help, of course, but if you rely on GPS and don't carry a map and compass, you will inevitably be tripped by Mr. Murphy, who will see to it that your batteries die or you drop the thing in a stream just when you need it.

Should your navigaion skills let you down or if you know where you are but run out of time to get out of the woods, you will need to concentrate on three things: fire for warmth, shelter, and water. Those skills will get you through the night and even through a couple of days. You will find all you need to know about those skills right here.

For most of us, survival skills are an insurance policy, one we hope we will never need. But when the sun drops and the temperature begins to fall and you find yourself in some cedar swamp five miles from the nearest road, you'll be very happy you're paid up on your premium. Enjoy your first installment!

—the Editors of *Field & Stream*

THE
FIELD & STREAM

Wilderness Survival Handbook

Introduction

Survival is the challenge of maintaining life in an environment capable of taking same. This really isn't a new concept to most folks, because the noisy mechanized jungle of modern civilization is at least as fraught with hazards as any wilderness; the conditions are just different. Almost every human today knows how to gauge the speed and flow of traffic before crossing a busy street, and few grow up without appreciating the dangers of electricity, natural gas, and power-driven appliances. As with every species since creation, our education in survival begins during infancy and stops only at death.

Unfortunately, our most familiar survival skills don't apply in a wilderness setting, where every year too many outdoorsmen (some of them professionals) run into trouble because they didn't recognize or expect the hazard they were about to encounter. A brain surgeon is no less intelligent in the woods than he is in the operating room, but the demands of life in nature are not the same as those in civilization, and a different set of skills is needed to meet them. It's hard to win any game when you don't know the rules by which it's played.

But it's also tough to learn these rules when you rarely get to play the game. The workaday world of mortgages, car payments, and dental appointments ensures that few lovers of nature can spend as much time enjoying it as they'd like. So learning the hard way, even if that were desirable, is pretty much out of the question. There are some mistakes you get to make only once.

That's where this book fits in, because our species alone possesses the ability—via the written word—to learn how to do something without ever having done it, or even having seen it done. Virtually anyone can bake a cake from scratch just by following the directions in a cookbook; I've applied the same principle to fire and shelter building, finding natural foods, and water purification. Experience will always be the best teacher, because it incorporates all your senses into accomplishing a task, but the survival "recipes" contained in these pages offer step-by-step procedures that almost anyone can reference and then implement, regardless of prior experience.

Much of the information in this book is generic in the sense that it can be used in all or most environments worldwide. For example, with just a modicum of inventiveness, the very efficient debris hut can be constructed as easily in the jungles of Burma as in a snowbound Canadian wilderness. And dangerous waterborne parasites are found in every freshwater river and lake on the planet, but all are dealt with using the same filtration and purification techniques.

Likewise, many of the survival skills described herein are applicable to urban environments, where you might find yourself suddenly without utilities and conveniences. It seems ironic that the most urgently needed commodity to be trucked in after a major flood is drinking water, and city dwellers are usually surprised to learn how many edible wild plants grow in vacant lots and up from sidewalk cracks. The intent here is to provide the information necessary to survive nearly any situation, from the aftermath of a natural disaster to finding your way back to civilization after a light-plane crash in the mountains.

More than that, this book has been heavily salted with useful tips and advice about avoiding things that are best not learned the hard way. Staying alive is the ultimate goal, but there's an awful lot of room for pain and suffering between life and death, and he who suffers the least usually survives the longest. If you hope to survive a bad situation, it makes no sense to hammer down your body's defenses through starvation, cold, or exhaustion. No human has ever been strong enough to face nature head-on, and it does no good to tough out 20 miles of a 30-mile hike in the rain if you wake up the next morning with bronchial pneumonia. In that vein, this book emphasizes survival skills that center on keeping warm, well fed, rested, and strong enough to endure the rigors that lie ahead.

Finally, this book blends time-honored and proven methods of survival with modern knives, compasses, and other tools that far surpass anything our forebears used. The loincloth-and-knife image of a survivalist makes for a great action movie, but the truth is that Tarzan, Rambo, and Mowgli are only fictional characters. Any human thrown naked and without tools into any wilderness environment is in real danger, and the more options you have for accomplishing any given task, the better your chances of survival under a variety of conditions will be. This is a book of options.

1

Orienteering

I can't rightly say I've ever been lost, but I've been
mighty perplexed for two or three days runnin'.
—Davy Crockett

Humans have no sense of direction. Like "lower" animals,
we have a ferric deposit at the tips of our noses, but our
species apparently lacks the sensory connections to make this biological magnet serve as an onboard compass. Modern science hasn't
quite comprehended the highly accurate biological compass found
in animals, but it appears that knowing the direction of magnetic
north is the basis for all navigational decisions.

Too, nearly all of a woodsman's orienteering calculations are
based on knowing in which direction north lies. The difference is
that, as when we're flying or breathing underwater, humans must
employ a machine to accomplish a task for which we have no natural ability. The most dependable tool available for this critical job
is a quality compass.

BASIC ORIENTEERING

How a Compass Works

A compass is the human solution to navigating unknown territories. The compass's rotating magnetized indicator is visibly drawn to the strongest magnet in the Northern Hemisphere: the magnetic north pole (the magnetic south pole if you're south of the equator). With a constant known point of reference, it becomes possible to follow a more or less straight course (terrain permitting) through the deepest wilderness. Each of us likes to believe we can do this without a compass, just by following our own judgment, but of the many who've tried—including myself—every one has walked in the proverbial circle a time or two.

Being magnetic, the indicator of every compass is attracted to ferric metals, so objects made from anything a magnet sticks to should be kept far enough from the compass to avoid affecting its indicator. Never try to take a bearing from inside or astride any vehicle; get at least 10 feet from all large metal objects. The knife on your hip won't cause a deflection, but I once saw a friend who knew better plotting a course with the compass lying in his palm, right next to his rifle barrel.

Indicator deflection is usually obvious from sluggish or erratic needle movements. A compass needle will naturally return to a north heading as it gets farther away from magnetic influences, but you should be aware that this can occur. The Huron mountain range in Michigan's Upper Peninsula is just one of many places where iron-rich rock magnetized by lightning can generate a field strong enough to make a compass indicator swing erratically, even completely around. Again, the source of magnetic influence is usually obvious, and the solution is to simply find another place where your compass behaves normally before "shooting" a bearing.

Aside from the deflection problem, every compass points to the same direction because it cannot do otherwise. There is no difference in "accuracy" between two functioning compasses, and no compass in good working order can be wrong. Doubting your compass is fairly common when you're traveling miles through unknown territory, but doing so is always a mistake. And attempting to compensate for the error you perceive is an even bigger mistake. I once hunted with a fellow who walked an extra 2 miles back to his truck after deciding that his compass was lying. Luckily his back trail crossed an abandoned railroad grade that was impossible to miss or he might easily have overshot our rendezvous point. Carry a good compass and trust it always.

The Compass Dial

Probably the most intimidating compass feature for an average beginner is its bezel, the numbered ring surrounding the indicator. The bezel is numbered to 360 degrees, which, you might recall, is the number of degrees in a complete circle. Divide this number by the four directions and you end up with quadrants, or fourths, that equal 90 degrees. Half of 360 is 180, which always equals the number of degrees of difference between the direction you're heading and the opposite way, also known as a back bearing or rear az-

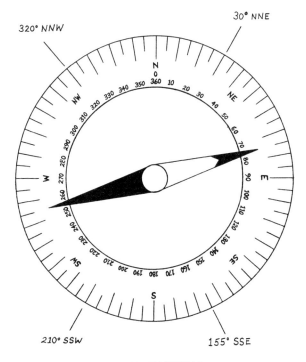

THE COMPASS DIAL

imuth. Going into the woods at a bearing of 275 degrees means the way back must be at a heading of 95 degrees (275 −180 = 95).

It might be easier to think of the compass bezel as a clock, except that in this case there are 360 degrees instead of 60 minutes. Both 360 (north) and 12 serve as both the start and end of their respective dials, with 3 o'clock equating to 90 degrees (east), 6 o'clock at 180 degrees (south), and 9 o'clock at 270 degrees (west).

Taking a Bearing

Probably the number one reason why folks get lost is failure to take a bearing before entering the woods. This isn't so critical if you've memorized the local terrain features and know the general direction of nearby roads, or if you're in open country where faraway landmarks constantly provide identifiable visual reference points. But in the forest, where visibility is often measured in yards, an initial bearing is vital. It's tough to determine which way leads out if you don't know which direction brought you in.

To take a bearing, lay the compass flat in your palm, horizontal to the earth. No compass works properly when held at an angle, because doing so causes the instrument's movement to bind. To work properly, every compass must be held or laid flat relative to the earth.

When your compass indicator settles and you're sure it isn't being deflected, align the N (360 degrees) on the compass bezel to the north—usually red—end of the indicator. With compass indicator and bezel correctly aligned to magnetic north, east is to its right, south to the rear, and west on the left. All you need to do then is use the bezel as a guide for maintaining a desired direction of travel.

When shooting an initial compass bearing, always try to reference your return to a hard-to-miss landmark. Even with a good compass, it's all but impossible to travel in a straight line through most untracked wilderness, be it mountain or swamp. And because a trekker must constantly alter course around natural obstacles, it isn't unusual to emerge from the woods 1/2 mile from where you had intended. Roads, rivers, railroad grades, and large lakeshores are all good, tough-to-miss target points, and I always try to fix their relative locations in my brain before entering an unexplored forest.

When you've established the direction you want to follow into the woods, you also know that the back bearing, or direction out, is

180 degrees away. A simple rule for calculating a back bearing is to subtract 180 from your direction of travel, or forward bearing, if that direction is greater than 180 degrees on the compass dial, and add 180 if the forward bearing is less than 180. If your direction of travel is at 70 degrees, the opposite direction will be at 250 degrees (70 + 180 = 250); if you're moving due west at 270 degrees, the way back will be at a heading of 90 degrees, or due east (270 − 180 = 90). Forward and back bearings must always equal 360 degrees when added together.

Maps

To get the most out of any compass you must complement it with a map of the area you'll be navigating. A compass can keep you on a steady course, but a map gives you a visual representation of the surrounding terrain. Having a preview of topographic features before reaching them allows a savvy orienteer to find water, identify landmarks, and avoid rough country while it's still far away.

Using map and compass together is simple: Spread the map flat on a level surface and lay your compass on top of it. Orient both map and compass to north and you'll have a miniaturized picture of the surrounding area. That trail the map shows to be south of your position is indeed south, and so on. Just determine your most likely location (explained in detail later), decide which landmark you'd like to reach, and then set off in the direction indicated by compass and map.

The Map Compass

While any compass can be used effectively with a map, some are better suited to the task than others, and a few have been specifically engineered to work with maps. Map compasses have a clear plastic base that allows them to be placed directly onto a map, which can then be read through the compass body.

The base of a map compass is etched with map scales that can also be superimposed over a map and read directly. These usually include the most commonly used map ratios, with straight edges graduated in inches and millimeters for use with all maps, and sometimes a protractor.

Better map compasses also sport a set of front and rear sights, much like a rifle or pistol, to make taking bearings from distant landmarks more precise. To use the sights, line them up on a landmark you want to reach or identify and hold them steady (this is the hard part) while you rotate the bezel's N (360 degrees) to the north end of the settled indicator. With bezel and indicator pointed north and the instrument's sights zeroed steadily on a distant point, the compass bearing to that point from your position will be the number that lines up with the front sight. The back, or reverse, bearing from that position to yours is shown at the rear sight. You don't even need to remember the numbers, because the bezel will hold its position, marking them while you use a map to determine how those bearings affect your course.

PRISMATIC MAP COMPASS

Most versatile of all map compasses are the relatively new prismatic models, which have a set of sights for zeroing in on identifiable landmarks and a flip-up mirror with a single vertical crosshair. Simply align the sights with a distant landmark, line up the mirror's crosshair to agree with both sights, and read its bearing, relative to your own position, at the top of the mirror. The back bearing from the landmark to your position will be marked simultaneously by the crosshair at the bottom of the mirror. You will have to read the numbers backward, of course, but with a little practice and tolerable conditions you'll be able take sight bearings with an error of less than 1 degree, which is insignificant in most situations.

ADVANCED ORIENTEERING

For most recreational outdoorsmen, in most instances just having the stable point of reference provided by a simple compass is sufficient to guarantee never getting lost. But finding your way back out of a wilderness doesn't require nearly as much precision as finding a single point inside a large woods does. A deer hunter who gets off course on the way out will likely face nothing tougher than a long walk back to his car, but a snowshoer who may be desperately seeking a backcountry cabin in howling snows cannot afford to miss by more than a few yards.

Two North Poles

Most deer hunters, mushroomers, and fishermen who venture off-trail into untracked woods need only know the direction of a

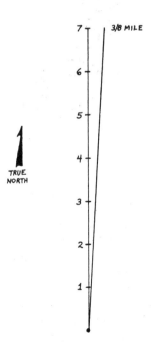

Effect of not compensating for a 3 degree declination
factor over a distance of 7 miles.

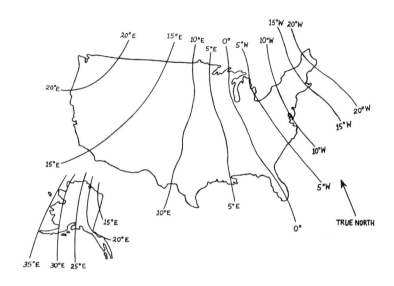

Effect of not compensating for a 3-degree declination
factor over a distance of 7 miles. Add the number of
degrees indicated on the map to your compass reading if
you are East of the zero declination line. Subtract if you
are West of the zero delination line.

road or well-marked trail, but multiple-day excursions over long
distances require a map.

The problem is that maps are typically oriented to true north,
a point that is actually 800 miles north of the magnetic north pole,
where all compasses point. Being offset means that there is only one
longitude where the two are in alignment, and the farther east or
west you travel from this line, the greater will be the disparity in
how the two norths line up with your geographic location. That disparity is called magnetic declination, or just declination, and is
measured in degrees.

In some locations, such as my home in northern Michigan, the
difference (3 degrees) is so slight that most day hikers can get by
with no compensation. But if you're in an untracked woods with no
regular landmarks to guide you, failure to account for a declination
of 3 degrees will put you off-course by more than a ¼ mile—enough
to completely miss a cabin in a storm. At the other extreme is

Alaska, with a disparity of more than 30 degrees that demands compensation for any trip farther than to an outhouse.

Correcting for magnetic declination is a simple matter of adding or subtracting the correct declination, in degrees, for the area you're traveling whenever you take a bearing. Begin by determining the approximate number of degrees your area varies from true north by referencing the declination map shown here. If you are east of the zero line, where the two norths are in alignment, add the number of degrees indicated on your compass to the number of degrees of declination. If you are west of the zero line, the number of degrees of declination will be subtracted from a compass heading to make it agree with a map oriented to true north.

TOPOGRAPHIC MAPS

A topographic, or contour, map differs from trail and road maps in that it uses concentric rings to illustrate heights and valleys, whereas the other types might show a 3,000-foot mountain as only a forested area. Having a trail map instead of a topo map in mountain country can seriously hinder your ability to navigate, because peaks and ridges that are clearly visible often do not appear on the map at all. It's much tougher to navigate around the base of a mountain and then pick up your course again on the other side when your map says there is no mountain there.

Reading a topographic map isn't as difficult as its maze of confusing lines and symbols makes it appear. A legend at the bottom of the map tells you at what scale the terrain shown is represented, and usually identifies the more common symbols used to show features such as bridges, marshes, and mineshaft tailings.

The contour lines themselves are even less complicated to decipher. The space between any two lines normally represents a difference in elevation of 10 feet between them (unless otherwise noted in the map's legend). Dark lines between lighter lines denote a rise or fall of 100 feet, so in a steady rise there will always be 10 lines (representing 10 feet apiece) from one dark line to the next. Differences in the distance between contour lines indicate how steeply the ground climbs between them. A rise of 30 feet over a linear space of 100 yards will result in contour lines that are much farther apart than a rise of 30 feet over a distance of just 10 feet. Since the latter change in elevation is considerably steeper than the former, contour lines denoting the difference in elevation will be much closer together. Noteworthy terrain features that occur between contour lines—such as pressure ridges and holes—are identified by dotted lines known as help lines.

Reading a Grid Map

Most area maps, and especially those intended for wilderness travel, are overlaid with a grid whose squares are scaled to precise distances. By knowing how much real distance in miles, kilometers, yards, or even inches a grid square represents, a hiker can directly measure how far it is from the river crossing he's just encountered to that night's campsite. Regardless of how faithfully a map might represent the terrain it covers, it has little use as a navigational reference if you can't use it to determine how far or wide the features shown there really are.

The most commonly used USGS scale is 1:24000, which means that 1 inch (one grid square) on the map represents 24,000 inches in real distance, or 2,000 feet. The entire United States has been mapped using this scale, and it is found on most map compasses.

A scale of 1:24000 is enough of a close-up of the area it covers to show smaller terrain features such as springheads, which makes it a good choice for maps used by research biologists who need great detail within a smaller area. But most folks seem more comfortable with a scale of 1:63360, which equates to 1 inch equals 1 mile of real distance on the map. 1:63360 maps can be ordered from the USGS (see chapter 1), and I recommend this scale for survival purposes because the slight loss of detail is more than offset by the greater geographic area covered per inch of map.

Keeping Track of Distances Traveled

Even with today's precision compasses and detailed topographic maps, any serious attempt at orienteering in a large wilderness requires some method for measuring and keeping track of distances traveled. Locating one tiny objective like a campsite or cabin in a forest can give real meaning to that old adage about finding a needle in a haystack. Without an ability to determine how far you've walked, it becomes difficult to calculate how far you still need to travel, or when to make a course change.

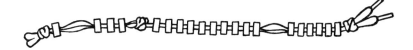

Top: Mile-type pace counter showing
distance traveled as 1 mile, 600 yards.
Bottom: Kilometer-type pace counter showing
distance traveled as 3 kilometers, 500 meters.

The simplest and most workable solution for keeping track of hiking distances is abacus-style pace counter used by the U.S. Army. These retail for about $5 at some army-navy outlets, but they're so simple to make that purchasing one seems a waste of money.

Construction of a pace counter is easy. Just thread 20 "beads" of ¼-inch I.D. (inside diameter) plastic fuel line, cut to ¼-inch lengths with a knife, onto a doubled shoelace. The beads fit snugly over the doubled shoelace, as they must, so you might need to pull the string through them with an awl or heavy wire. With all 20 beads threaded onto the shoelace, tie a single overhand knot on each end to prevent them from slipping free, then segregate the beads into groups of 4 and 16 with another knot in the string's center. The pace counter is ready for use.

To use the pace counter, first determine how many normal steps you must take to cover 100 yards. The army has determined that 100 yards equals 62 paces for an average man, but since people differ and the accuracy of your pace counter depends largely on knowing how many steps will cover 100 yards, it pays to use your own stride length rather than this arbitrary formula.

For example, my own stride is almost exactly 3 feet, and actual measurements have revealed only about 1 foot of error in 100 yards, so I calculate 100 steps as 100 yards. Beginning with all beads pushed to its center, I slide 1 bead from the larger group to the end for every 100 yards walked. When all 17 beads have been pushed to the outside end, 1,700 yards will have passed, just shy of the 1,760 yards in a mile. At this point all beads in the larger group are "reset" by pushing them back to the string's center, and 1 bead from the smaller group is pushed to that end, denoting passage of 1 mile. Repeat the process until all 5 of the mile beads have been pushed to the end (5 miles). I like to try to verify my location at this point, or you can simply reset all the beads to the center and go another 5 miles.

Vectoring a Position

We'd been bouncing along the rutted and rocky century-old truck trail at a breakneck speed of 5 miles per hour for more than three hours when my companions and I decided to give our battered kidneys a break and stop for the night. The problem was that nearly

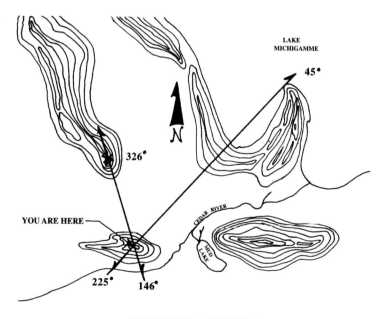

VECTORING A POSITION

all of our driving had been through low, heavily forested mountains, and we had only a vague idea of where we were on a map.

The easiest way to determine where you are in a wilderness is a technique known as vectoring, which essentially means using the position of two landmarks that can be positively identified as references to your own position. In some cases, including the one just described, this means climbing to an elevated location from which you can see the surrounding terrain features, but I've also vectored my position using identifiable peninsulas and other landmarks on lakes or other open places.

First, locate two landmarks that can be recognized both from the countryside and on your map. Shoot a bearing (described earlier) to one of them, jotting down its relative bearing in degrees in the margin of your map. Do the same with the other reference point.

Once you've established the bearing of both landmarks from your own position, the next step is to calculate the back bearing from these points to your position, or 180 degrees in the opposite direction. If the bearing to one of these reference landmarks is 320 degrees, and the other 145 degrees, then the back bearings will be 140 degrees and 325 degrees, respectively.

The final step is transferring these numbers to your map. Orient the map and compass to north, then, using the compass bezel as a protractor, extend a line from the first landmark at an angle of 140 degrees. Extend another line from the second landmark at an angle of 325 degrees. You'll note that at one point the lines intersect one another to form an X. The junction of this X denotes your location on the map.

Some folks prefer to triangulate their coordinates, which differs from vectoring only in that it employs three identifiable landmarks as opposed to two. Ideally, all three lines should cross at the same point, but in reality they usually form a triangle. The center of that triangle is where you are.

NATURAL COMPASSES

While it would be foolish to deny yourself the advantages afforded by a compass and detailed map, it's also true that Native peoples around the world have been successfully navigating long distances without either for many millennia. Humans might never have had a sense of direction, but we've always had the sense needed to use natural indicators of direction. As long as you have one reliable and known point of reference, you are never lost, and nature has provided several.

Wind

Prevailing winds are often a good indicator of direction. Warm summer winds across North America are always from the southeast, which explains why its eastern coastline is hurricane country in summer. Winter winds are out of the northwest, as evidenced by animated weather maps that always show storm fronts traveling southeast across America.

While wind direction is actually a pretty reliable seasonal compass, the old trick of wetting a finger and determining direction from which side feels coolest is not to be trusted. The problem is that only prevailing winds, those high up in the jet stream that drive the clouds, can be counted on to blow as described. Terrain features make winds in low-lying areas unpredictable, channeling air currents through trees, valleys, and around hills until the breeze might blow steadily from a direction opposite that of the prevailing winds. "Swampers" who hunt deer inside their own bedding grounds disregard the always-stay-downwind rule because they know breezes there blow from every direction, and a few have made an art of using this phenomenon to confuse and then ambush a whitetail.

Trees

Trees are an often-overlooked indicator of direction in the North, where sometimes-vicious winter winds from the northwest kill or severely stunt branches exposed to the brunt of their fury. Most susceptible are tall pines and spruces that extend above the forest canopy, but often lone pines at the edge of open water or prairies will also be barren on their northwestern sides. Aside from being good indicators of direction, because the longest and healthiest branches point generally southward, these trees serve as examples of why veteran backpackers take to the lowland woods, like deer, when a cold wind blows.

Sun

The sun passes from east to west across the southern horizon from anywhere in the Northern Hemisphere. The farther north you

travel, the more southerly will be the sun's daily pass across the sky. In the Southern Hemisphere the sun also crosses the sky east to west, but there it will be in the northern sky. Only at the equator, where the sun is directly overhead, will our star not be in the southern sky from anywhere north.

Although the sun has guided humans through the wilderness for millennia, it is not to be relied on, only referred to from time to time. Dense forest or just a cloudy day can make it impossible to see even a glow from the sun, so don't leave the compass behind.

Moon

Like our sun, the moon rises in the east and crosses to the west as night evolves into day, and in summer it's possible to see both rising sun and setting moon at the same time. Also like our sun, the moon makes its nightly passage in the southern sky when viewed from anywhere in the Northern Hemisphere. Heading straight for a risen moon at the apex of its trajectory (usually after midnight) means that you're walking south.

Again, the moon is not to be relied on, only used for confirmation from time to time. For about one week out of each month there will be a new moon, which so far as a wilderness trekker is concerned means nights that are inky black, even when skies are clear and star filled. A full moon might also be hidden by forest canopy or clouds.

Stars

I've never had much talent for picking the shapes of people and animals from among the billions of stars that fill a nighttime sky in the wilderness. Perhaps I've just neglected some part of my brain, but I can't see most constellations even when an astronomy buff points them out.

However, some are obvious even to me, and these have been of considerable use to me for navigating at night.

The Big Dipper (Ursa Major) and Little Dipper (Ursa Minor), or Big Bear and Little Bear, are perhaps the most identifiable star formations in the Northern Hemisphere at night. In summer both sit high in the sky, the Big Dipper above and to the left (west) of the Little Dipper. The dippers face each other, with Ursa Major's handle pointing almost straight upward and the Little Dipper's handle pointed downward. The bright star at the end of the Little Dipper's handle is Polaris, the North Star, which—true to its name—is a reliable indicator of that direction.

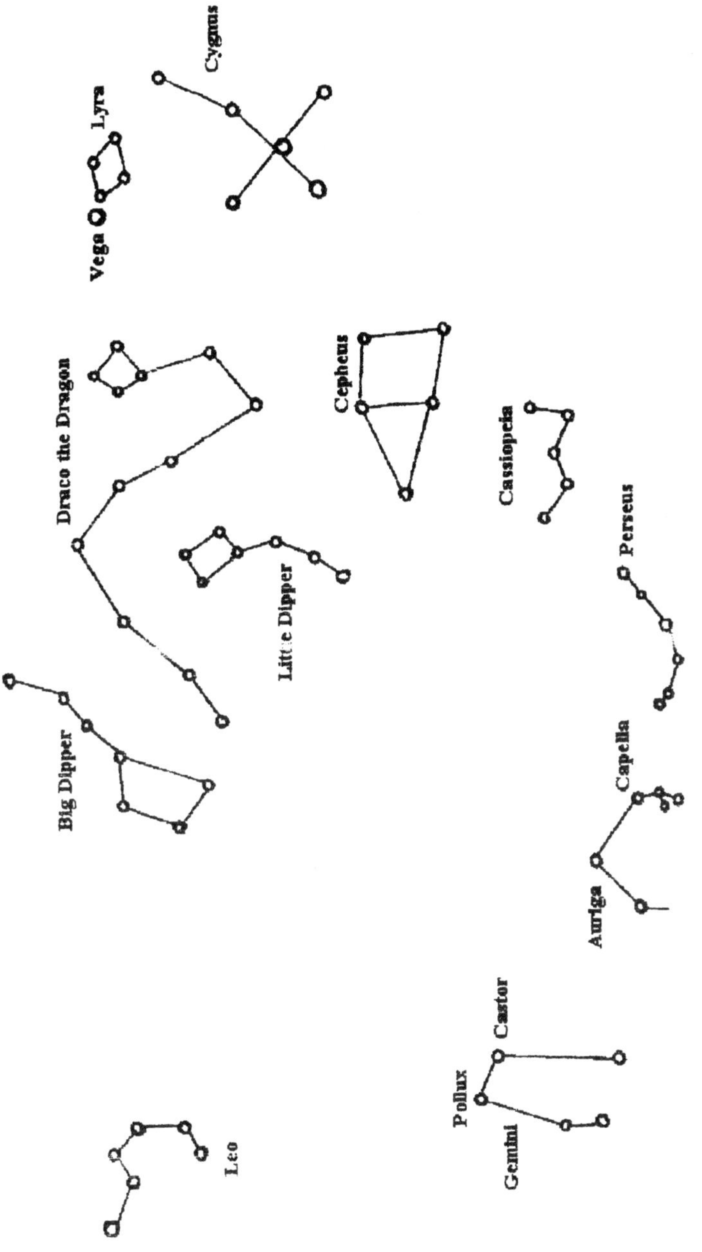

THE SUMMER NIGHT SKY, LOOKING NORTH

Cygnus

Lyra

Vega

Draco the Dragon

Cepheus

Cassiopeia

Little Dipper

Perseus

Big Dipper

Capella

Auriga

Castor

Pollux

Gemini

Leo

23

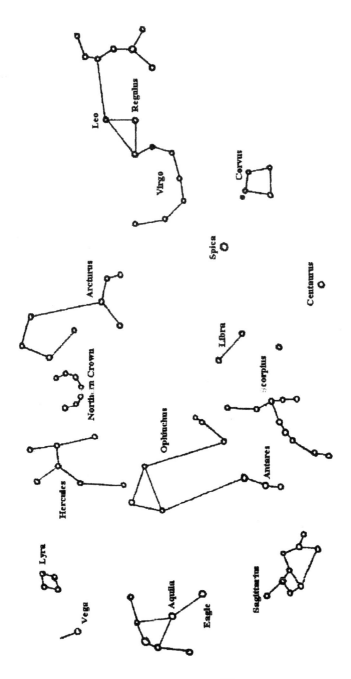

THE SUMMER NIGHT SKY, LOOKING SOUTH

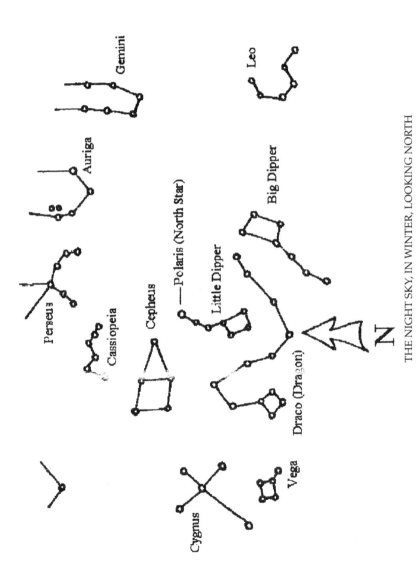

Gemini

Leo

Auriga

Polaris (North Star)

Big Dipper

Perseus

Little Dipper

Cassiopeia

Cepheus

Draco (Dragon)

N

Cygnus

Vega

THE NIGHT SKY, IN WINTER, LOOKING NORTH

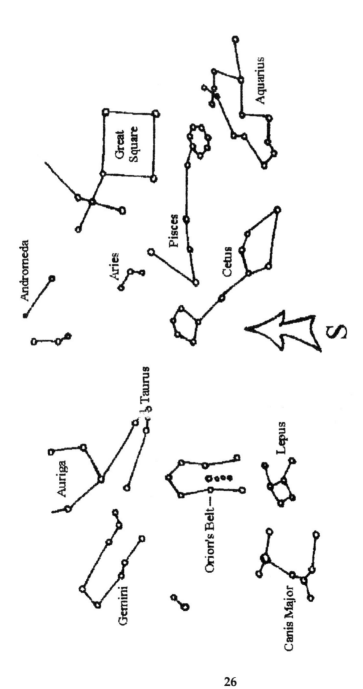

THE NIGHT SKY, IN WINTER, LOOKING SOUTH

26

In winter the dippers are still in the northern night sky but reversed, with the Big Dipper right (east), its handle extending nearly to earth. Ursa Minor's handle points straight upward and is again tipped with the North Star.

Orion's Belt is another obvious star formation that has served as a valuable reference, especially in winter, when this bright row of three stars is most visible in the southern sky. Supposedly the belt of Orion the Hunter, which I can't recognize, these stars range at a slight diagonal from the lower left to the upper right, and are easily picked out from other, less bright stars. When you're walking toward Orion's Belt, you're headed generally south.

Moss

I feel obligated to cover the topic of moss on the sides of trees, and whether or not it can be used to indicate direction. The old saw claims that moss, a shade- and moisture-loving plant, will tend to the northerly sides of tree trunks in a forest, away from the sun, which was always in the southern sky for American pioneers.

In fact, mosses grow where they can, in the conditions that most favor their survival and regardless of direction. In the permanent twilight of a mature cedar swamp, moss will likely surround the tree trunks where it grows. In a mature hardwood forest, where large, strong trees and a thick overhead canopy prevent new growth from below, moss is likely to be found growing only on the southerly sides of trees, driven there by cold winds from the northwest in winter. And if conditions are just right for moss to seek protection from sunlight on the north sides of trunks and stumps, well, then you'll have the sun as a guide.

2

Making and
Using Fire

Fire was the first of the elements to be bent to mankind's will, and mastery of it gave comparatively godlike power to an omnivorous scavenger who had previously lived in fear of meat eaters that were faster, stronger, and better armed. All other beasts feared fire, which meant that our early ancestors were able to sleep, socialize, and imagine in a state of relaxation never enjoyed by other species. With fire, the law of the jungle no longer applied to humans; our kind had successfully removed itself from the natural food chain.

In the light, warmth, and safety provided by a crackling fire, primeval man learned how to paint likenesses of what he had seen onto convenient stone walls. These simple pictures eventually evolved into written languages that allowed young Abraham Lincoln to read by hearth light and Albert Einstein to explain the most frightening power source yet discovered. In a relatively short time our species learned to harden clay, forge metals, make glass, kill parasites in food, and finally bake microcomputer chips, all by means of fire.

Mastery of fire can be every bit as important to a modern human as it was to our prehistoric ancestors, because there are few places on earth that don't get cold or wet enough to cause hypothermia during some months of every year. To humans, ambient temperatures of 50 degrees F or less are potentially life threatening, whether they occur in Alaska or Bermuda. Throw in a steady rain and the cooling effect that being wet has on the body, and air temps feel 20 degrees colder. Add a brisk wind, and any human not properly dressed or inside shelter is in real danger. As any deep-water sailor can attest, even an 80-degree day can be downright cold when you're wet and windblown.

TINDER MATERIALS

Presuming you have an adequate fire-starting tool in hand (see chapter 1), the first step in making fire is gathering tinder. Tinder is essentially any easily ignited combustible material that will produce flames of sufficient heat and duration to ignite small twigs. Fortunately, there are many natural and man-made materials that work well for this most critical stage in the fire-making process.

Birch Bark

Birch bark is the classic north woodsman's tinder material, especially the scroll-like bark of the white, or paper, birch. Native to moist forests across the northern United States, Canada, and throughout Alaska, white, yellow, and silver birches are easily identified by small rolls of dead bark curling away horizontally from their trunks. Bark from yellow and silver birches also works well as tinder, though it's typically coarser and harder to light.

Despite concerns from environmentalists, any birch bark you can peel free using only your hands is essentially that tree's equivalent of hair or fingernails, and stripping it off does the tree no harm at all. Never cut into the bark to remove it, because if the tree is stripped down to its brown cambium layer, it will nearly always die.

Already-dead birch logs lying on the ground are another matter. Birch bark is tough and able to withstand exposure to the elements for several years, but the wood beneath it quickly decays to a wet powder. By stabbing your knife into such a rotting log then drawing the cutting edge lengthwise through the bark, the entire log can be peeled into a single, large section of bark that work as well for shingling a shelter roof or leaving a wilderness note scrawled in charcoal as it does for starting a fire.

In dry weather birch bark can be taken from the ground, but in a hard rain it quickly becomes apparent that birch bark isn't nearly as waterproof as its reputation indicates. That's why birch-bark canoes were always pulled ashore and turned upside down each night. When bark from the ground becomes too waterlogged to ignite, curls of the stuff stripped from standing trees will usually have remained dry enough to burn.

Igniting birch bark is most easily accomplished by applying a match or lighter flame to the thinnest portion of the strip until it catches and becomes self-sustaining. If your fire-starting tool is a spark thrower, ignition is best accomplished by first stripping a section of bark into a pile of very thin ribbons.

Lichens

Reindeer moss (*Cladonia rangiferina*) is not only one of the most nutritious—if unpalatable—wild foods found around the world, but it's also an excellent fire starter when dry. Fond of open, sunny places and sandy soils, this lichen is easily identified as carpetlike growths of green, gray, or bluish masses that few other plants can penetrate.

When reindeer moss is dry enough to crunch to powder underfoot, it's also highly flammable and will ignite with the touch of a flame. When rain, dew, or melting snow cause these absorbent carpets to become spongy with absorbed moisture, they will not burn.

Grasses

Dead, brown grasses are found the world over, particularly along the shorelines of rivers, lakes, and ponds, and as anyone who's seen them burn can tell you, all are extremely flammable when dry.

When gathering dead grasses, always wear gloves, because the abrasive leaves of many species have edges sharp enough to slice unprotected skin. Gathering then becomes a matter of crooking and spreading your fingers to form a rake, then scraping the dead stalks from live ones and into a pile.

Dry grass ignites with either flame or spark, burning hot for a short duration. Damp grasses are less combustible, and may tend to smolder, requiring you to blow gently into the glowing tinder pile to keep it flaming.

Pine Needles and Sap

Dry pine needles are dangerously flammable when they lie in carpets under their parent trees, and are probably responsible for more accidental forest fires than any other natural material. All evergreens contain a flammable sap within their needles, and while some, like the white pine, are very fine and more easily lit than others, all of them will burn at the touch of a spark. Prolonged exposure to water can leave them too wet to light easily, but pine needles are among the most water resistant of nature's tinders.

Pine sap becomes a hard resin when dried, and clumps of it have historically been melted onto cloth tied to the end of a stick, or even onto brown cattail heads, where it serves as a slow-burning torch. Pine pitch also makes a good fire starter when melted onto the end of a dry twig then lit like a match. Pine sap is of course found most often on pine trees of all species, where clumps of the stuff are exuded from woodpecker and grub wounds to coagulate and harden on the outer bark.

Fibrous Bark

Although less famous than birch, the dry inner bark of dead aspen and poplar trees contains a fibrous layer that separates into strands when the more brittle outer bark is broken away. These strands can be woven into rope, if necessary, but their best use is as fire-starting tinder. Dry fibers ignite at the touch of a match, and even damp inner-bark strands can be coaxed into a self-sustaining blaze with a little work.

STARTING A FIRE

Making fire is a process. It's a task comprised of many smaller tasks that help ensure a warm, crackling blaze with a minimum of time and effort, without frustration and time-consuming false starts. In everyday conditions it may not seem important to start a fire swiftly and surely, but if you find yourself backpacking in an unseasonable freezing rain, the tools and skills needed to make fire quickly can be vital.

The first step is to site your fire so that its flames won't be dissipated or accidentally spread to the surrounding foliage by wind. Lakeshores, prairies, and rocky outcrops are poor places to make a campfire, while gullies and ravines are among the best.

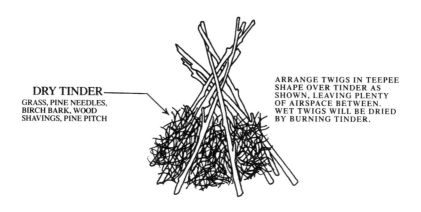

DRY TINDER
GRASS, PINE NEEDLES,
BIRCH BARK, WOOD
SHAVINGS, PINE PITCH

ARRANGE TWIGS IN TEEPEE
SHAPE OVER TINDER AS
SHOWN, LEAVING PLENTY
OF AIRSPACE BETWEEN.
WET TWIGS WILL BE DRIED
BY BURNING TINDER.

STARTING A CAMPFIRE—TEPEE METHOD

The next step is to excavate a shallow fire pit, about 4 inches deep by 2 feet in diameter, and pile excavated soil into a low wall around the pit's perimeter. Besides the obvious advantage of keeping stray embers to a minimum, a fire pit is also more efficient for cooking because heat is radiated onto cooking vessels from all sides.

In most places the dirt removed from your fire pit will be damp, which means that a fire placed atop it will be hampered by the cooling effects of rising steam until all moisture has evaporated. To overcome this problem, especially in wet weather or on top of snow, I first lay a fire bed of dry twigs and branches placed side by side at the pit's bottom. The fire bed keeps the fledgling coals from making direct contact with and being cooled by the damp earth below, resulting in less time from spark to blaze.

Firewood

Wherever you build a campfire it will have to be fed, and the availability of burnable dead trees or brush is sometimes a prerequisite to selecting a suitable semipermanent base camp site. Keeping a fire hot enough to keep you warm against a chilly night will consume considerable fuel, more as temperatures get colder. Laying in a good supply of firewood is high on the list of priorities when settling into a campsite each evening; you really don't want to be stumbling through tangled forest with a heavy load of firewood after dark, not even with a flashlight.

Firewood is a bit different in the backcountry. Rotting wood, even the wet stuff lying on a forest floor, is acceptable fuel once you've established a hot bed of coals below. In fact, damp decaying logs can be used to keep a fire slowly smoldering for a day or more, and for sending daylight rescue signals.

Dead is the word to keep in mind when gathering firewood from a natural environment. Aside from the obvious ethical implications, cutting live trees is far too much work, and nature has seen to it that even green twigs contain too much moisture to create a self-sustaining blaze. Green wood doesn't work as firewood.

Likewise, deadwood lying on the forest floor is likely to be damp and decaying on the bottom, but if your fire has a good bed of coals, even these will dry quickly and burn.

The best prospects for firewood in a forest are dead standing trees and wind-downed limbs that didn't quite fall to the ground. Being surrounded by open air, these will always be the driest fuel available, and a single downed tree can provide everything from tinder to long-burning "night logs" for the cool hours between sunset and bedtime.

For this reason, it pays to look upward for firewood rather than picking it off the forest floor. Dead standing trees are easy to spot among live branches, and a hard push against their trunks is often all that's required to bring them down as firewood. Do watch for "widowmaker" tops and branches that might break off independently and come crashing down.

There are also no precut logs to burn in the backcountry, and despite the availability of some very good camp saws, cutting firewood into neat lengths is simply not a good bargain in terms of calories expended. An old woodcutter's proverb states that every stick of firewood heats up a body twice, providing a little heat during the burning, and a lot of heat during the cutting.

The easiest solution is to burn uncut any long pieces of wood that are too heavy to break. Lay the center of the length across your fire, adding smaller pieces of wood as needed to maintain coals. When the length burns in half, slide the two burned ends into the fire a foot or so at a time until they're gone.

USING FIRE

Once you've made a fire, the next step is to make it work for you. With fire, you can withstand the coldest temperatures, cook foods to kill parasites, signal for help, sterilize water for drinking, and see at night. Without fire, all of these simple tasks range from difficult to impossible.

The Heating Fire

Heat is probably the most important reason to have fire in a survival situation, because while it takes months to die of starvation and days to die of thirst, a few hours of cold rain without protective clothing or warmth can be fatal.

Beginning with a hot bed of coals, you can maximize the heat radiated from a fire by placing all lengths of wood side by side atop

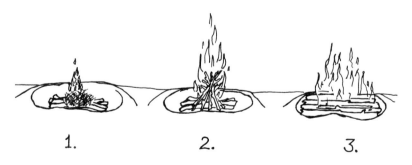

THE THREE STEPS IN CAMPFIRE-BUILDING.
1. LIT TINDER IN EXCAVATED FIRE PIT. 2. TEPEE
OF KINDLING. 3. WORKING CAMPFIRE OF SIDE-
BY-SIDE LENGTHS OF FIREWOOD THAT FORM A
STABLE COOKING PLATFORM.

PROPER FIRE PIT

the embers. This method allows large pieces of firewood to be stacked lengthwise atop one another, pyramid style, forming a low wall that not only burns hotly but also acts to reflect heat back toward whomever is seated before it.

Likewise, having some sort of wall at your back while seated before a fire will act to reflect heat that would otherwise be lost. This reflector can be a tarp erected on a a framework of branches, but in most terrain you'll be able to find a gully or hill whose face will serve even better. Placing your body between fire and reflector greatly increases the amount of felt heat by surrounding you with radiated warmth.

Cooking Fires

Like making a fire, cooking over an open fire is a skill that most folks don't find the need to practice very often. The most common frustration encountered by campfire cooks is burned food, because a campfire is several times hotter than any kitchen range, and it heats a cooking vessel from all sides.

The trick to cooking over fire lies in controlling the heat that it passes to your cooking pot. It also helps to have the cooking vessel seated on a stable surface that won't suddenly give way and send your meal spilling onto the ground. Both of these problems are remedied with a cooking platform.

First, the fire must be made ready for cooking. You'll need to start with a hot bed of coals that will provide steady heat to wood placed on top, which means the fire will have burned for a half hour or so before it's ready.

When a bed of hot coals has been generated, push any burning wood on the coals to one side with a stick, then scrape the embers flat with the same stick. Finally, lay a relatively neat and even platform of same-diameter sticks side by side on top of the coals. The platform will immediately begin to smolder, and within two or three minutes you should have tongues of flame licking upward from between the sticks. Place your cooking pot on this platform, pushing downward firmly against its rim with a rocking motion to ensure that the cooking platform is flat against the coals and the pot is flat and secure on top. If more wood is needed to complete the cooking process, simply remove the cooking vessel, lay more sticks directly on top of the depleted platform, and replace the vessel, repeating the seating process.

Trench Stove

A trench stove is the original camp stove, and one I've used many times in places or situations where a hot meal was desirable but the smoke, flame, and inconvenience of extinguishing a conventional cooking fire were not. As its name implies, this cooking tool begins with a narrow trench, about 3 or 4 inches wide by 10 inches long by 6 inches deep, dug into whatever soil is available. One or both ends of the trench should be angled downward from the surface to better facilitate adding fuel to the fire below.

Unlike a camp cooking fire, the trench stove requires no preparation and no coals. Simply build a small fire at the bottom of the trench and set your cooking pot across it so that both sides rest securely on the ground, leaving the pot's center exposed to the fire. Small, pencil-sized twigs fed in from the trench ends as needed keep the small flame burning hotly, which also helps minimize the amount of smoke and odor generated in a place where either might alert potential prey.

Perhaps the best feature of a trench stove is that it can be quickly erased after use, leaving no sign that a fire ever burned there. Just shove the dirt excavated from the trench during construction back into the hole, smothering the small fire instantly. Leaves and forest debris sprinkled on top of the refilled trench work to make it indistinguishable from the rest of the forest floor, if this is a concern.

Signal Fires

Fire is a lost or injured outdoorsman's best chance for attracting the attentions of rescuers, or even folks who aren't actively looking for someone in distress. As one outdoor TV show host told me, "My plan for getting rescued is to build a great big goddamned fire and wait for someone to come and get me." Simple as that sounds, it's a pretty good strategy.

Signal fires are by definition intended to be visible from long distances. At night a bright, blazing fire can be seen from many miles, especially from the air, so the means to create this signal should be kept at hand in the form of a hot coal bed whenever a hopeful rescuee makes camp.

Because burning a brightly flaming fire all night long isn't practical in terms of wood and energy expended, campfires are best maintained at a manageable working size for cooking and warmth, then quickly stoked when needed as a signal. This means keeping a ready supply of fast-burning tinder and kindling close at hand and dry every evening.

Better yet, depending on the terrain, is a dedicated signal fire sited in a high, open place where it will be visible from as far away as possible. Basically a giant version of the tepee used for starting a fire, a signal fire consists of a half-dozen 6-foot poles of deadwood tied together a foot below their tops then spread at their bottoms to form a freestanding frame. A smaller tepee of tinder and kindling laid on the ground inside the larger tepee frame is protected from wind and rain, ready to light with a spark.

Be aware that a tepee signal fire will flame quickly if laid correctly, becoming too hot to approach closely, and it will eventually fall over when enough supports are burned away. The last thing an injured backpacker needs is to run from a forest fire of his own making, so site your signal fire carefully and clear away any combustible debris for at least 10 feet all around.

The Coal Bed

When one of my survival students inevitably asks how I would handle a cold night without my bedroll, I show them the coal bed, or hot bed. This ancient method of providing yourself with a warm place to get a restful night's sleep has doubtless saved the lives of many trappers and mountain men. I can only say with certainty that it has made a lot of cold winter nights in the woods downright tolerable for my companions and me.

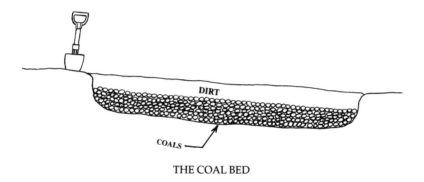

THE COAL BED

The coal bed starts with a body-size excavation at least 8 inches deep in whatever loose soil is available. Your survival knife will probably be crucial to the process of chopping through roots and loosening packed dirt, especially if the ground is frozen. Hard-frozen earth may have to first be thawed, and this is most easily accomplished by building a body-length fire atop the site to be excavated. When this thawing fire has burned down to a hot bed of coals, the dirt below will have been softened enough to dig through.

Next, scrape the hot coals to one side with a slab of wood or rock and excavate the depression that will serve as your bed. Pile the dirt to one side and push the mound of coals into the hole. Rebuild a hot fire in its bottom, spreading hot coals over the length and width until the depression contains a layer of them at least 2 inches deep. Refill the hole with dirt and pack it down firmly with your feet.

Simply not having the earth absorb your body heat during sleep is a real advantage in itself, but a coal bed actively generates warmth for 6 to 10 hours, depending on how thick a layer of coals you use. If the weather is very cold and you have no bedroll, excavate an extra 4 inches of dirt for use in covering your entire body like a blanket.

The obvious danger posed by a coal bed is that of getting burned, but if your bed is deep enough and covered by at least 4 inches of packed soil, this shouldn't be a problem. And if circumstances dictate that you must remain in one place for several consecutive days, loosened cover soil can be re-excavated from the bed and reused again and again until available wood runs out or warmer weather arrives.

Banking a Fire

Anyone who uses a campfire will eventually leave it unattended for some period of time, and if you're in a genuine survival dilemma you'll definitely want a fire to keep burning while you're gathering food or performing other necessary chores. Leaving a campfire unattended should never be considered under ordinary circumstances, but when it must be done, it should be done correctly to negate any possibility of a wildfire.

The practice of reducing a fire to an idle that neither burns nor dies out is called banking. Hot coals at the bottom of the fire pit are almost entirely covered by a platform of large, damp, half-rotted logs placed side by side atop them. Fed by the very logs that keep them mostly smothered, coals will smolder overnight, ready to be coaxed into fire again when needed. Gusts of wind cannot spread the contained embers, and nothing short of a torrential rain will extinguish them. If neglected for too long a time, the coals will burn into the bottoms of the banking logs until a growing gap between coals and fuel causes the fire to die from starvation.

3

Shelter

All animals seek out some form of shelter against the elements, for protection from natural enemies, and to rear their vulnerable young. Beavers build lodges, marmots excavate earthen dens, and deer yard up in deep lowland swamps where cold winds don't penetrate. Few animals willingly suffer exposure to inclement weather, because cooling wind, rain, or snow places undue stress on an animal's metabolism, forcing it to expend more energy to maintain normal body temperature.

Previous generations feared the elements, as evidenced by old adages like "Come inside before you catch your death of pneumonia," or "He doesn't have enough sense to come in from the rain." These frontier proverbs are still repeated today, but for most people they no longer carry the same dark meaning they had in the days before antibiotics, when pneumonia was mostly untreatable and too often fatal.

But if you're in a survival situation, you should take these old sayings as gospel, because you'll be facing the same exposure and lack of medical attention that struck fear into the hardiest voyageur or mountain man of old. Under such conditions a shelter from the proverbial storm could become downright imperative, so it pays to have as many options as possible. Following are several of the most effective and easily constructed shelters for a variety of weather conditions.

BASIC SHELTER MATERIALS

Plastic sheeting, or verathane, like that used to cover lumber and other equipment against rain or dew, has been a part of my backwoods survival kit since I was a boy. Many rainy summer nights I would simply spread an approximately 10- by 10-foot sheet over my bedroll like a giant blanket and sleep soundly while raindrops spattered harmlessly against my plastic shield and were absorbed into the surrounding earth. Because the plastic is held up by grasses and foliage, it never actually touches the ground, so danger from suffocation is nil. Throwing the sheet over a low shrub increases ventilation and provides more elbow room while gear, dead wood, rocks, or other weighty objects anchor its edges against the wind.

You can also turn a sheet of verathane into an improvised pup tent by tying a cord between two trees then draping the plastic across it evenly. A slipknot of cord tightened around bunched-up plastic at the corners provides the means to tie these corners to stakes whittled from available wood.

In rainy weather, a sheet of verathane can work as a gear shelter if you stretch it between four trees and tie off the corners to trunks and branches several feet above the ground. This shelter's entry should be tied off at least a foot higher than its rear to form a sloped roof that leaves no place for collected water to pool—sort of an elevated lean-to. It can also serve as a quickly erected rain shelter should you be deluged by a sudden cold rain.

While it can serve as a shelter by itself, a sheet of verathane carried rolled up into a tight cylinder and wrapped with several yards of nylon cord provides the handiest way to construct waterproof field shelters. Like the poles of a tent, a frame made from readily available branches or dead saplings can support and hold the plastic in whatever configuration you can create from a given environment.

Verathane can be purchased in rolls of varying lengths and widths from most lumberyards and home supply stores, but I've scrounged some large cast-off pieces from construction sites. Available colors are usually black, opaque, or clear, and I usually recommend the latter two because they are more easily seen from the air in summer, and because they allow sunlight to penetrate when used as a solar condensation still. I suggest getting the heaviest mil thickness you can find, backed up by a partial roll of duct tape for patching holes in the field.

Space (or emergency) Blankets also have a place in the survival kit, and are in fact superior to verathane because their foil-laminated Mylar construction not only is waterproof but also acts as a giant mirror when spread as a shelter roof. If the objective is to be rescued, a Space Blanket lean-to tied between trees so that it faces south (north if you're south of the equator) will reflect sunlight all day toward any aircraft flying south of your position.

IMPROVISED SHELTERS

No environment on earth completely lacks the means to construct an effective long- or short-term survival shelter from the surrounding terrain. Sod-buster farmers who settled North America's Great Plains coped with a lack of timber by building their notably bullet- and fireproof houses with bricks of sod cut from the prairie. Eskimo igloos convert ice and snow taken from the coldest, most hostile places on earth into a comparatively cozy refuge against these very elements. From sandstone pueblos and cedar-bark hogans to the clay roofing tiles of Mexican haciendas, humans have always found their own means of escaping the elements.

Lean-To Shelter

This is the classic survival shelter of movies and novels. In its simplest form a lean-to is just a flat, rainproof roof suspended several feet above ground at its entrance, and sloping downward to the earth at its rear. The flat roof provides a good reflector for directing heat radiated by a campfire back onto the shelter's occupant while also protecting him from the cooling effects of rain and wind.

A quick-and-dirty lean-to can be created by tying a tarp or plastic sheet between two trees about 4 feet up, then staking or tying the opposite two corners closer to the ground, as described earlier, to give it a sloping roof. A more classic construction is to suspend a horizontal crossbar of dead but sturdy wood about 4 feet up by tying it onto tree trunks or (my preference) setting each end into convenient

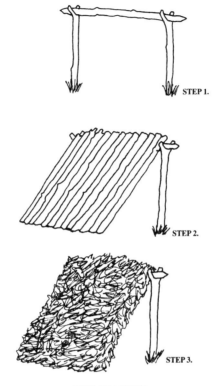

STEP 1.

STEP 2.

STEP 3.

THE LEAN-TO

crotches between adjacent trees. With a strong horizontal support in place, you can then add a roof frame of long dead branches and saplings whose upper ends lie across the main support while their opposite ends rest on the ground. Keep placing long branches across the main support at about the same angle until you've created a sloping platform from the main support to the ground.

As you'll see for yourself, this sloping roof of branches and saplings is not watertight, or even windproof, so the next step is to add a kind of shingle layer to keep out the wind and rain that will keep you from sleeping well. My favorite among natural materials is the almost ubiquitous bracken fern, which is a common summer sight in forests throughout North America. A layer of overlapping bracken fronds placed from bottom to top over the roof and held in place by a half-dozen heavy saplings provides a fairly watertight cover. Leaf debris from the forest floor also works for plugging holes, but, as with other survival shelters, the quickest and most waterproof roofing material is a lightweight tarp or sheet of verathane.

Debris Shelter

This is the first shelter I teach my survival students to build, because some form of it can be easily constructed in almost any wooded environment, without tools, cord, or even skill. The materials used consist solely of deadwood and foliage taken from the surrounding area and used to construct a shelter you could call home indefinitely. I lived in a large debris shelter for two months while researching my book, *The Complete Tracker,* and once used a low body-size debris shelter to weather two days in a blizzard that made roads impassable to even snowmobiles. The beauty of this shelter is the way it uses snow accumulation as insulation in winter, yet remains a comparatively cool source of shade against a hot sun.

Every debris shelter begins with a stout center pole, preferably a dead and dry, but not rotted, sapling that's too strong to be broken under your body weight. Its length should be about 9 feet to ensure that the completed shelter will be long enough to comfortably accommodate your prone body.

Wedge the butt, or thicker, end of the center pole into a tree crotch about 4 feet above the earth. The narrow end of the pole should always be on the ground, because it would be the first part to break should the shelter's roof become overloaded with snow and ice. You'll note that the center pole creates a triangle between itself, the supporting tree, and the ground. All of the construction in a debris hut makes use of angles, friction, and gravity to give it the strength and longevity of some houses.

With the center pole in place, you can now add the walls. These are fashioned simply by leaning branches, or any suitably long pieces of wood, side by side between the center pole and the ground. The higher entrance end will of course require longer wall members than the lower foot end, but in a half hour or so you'll have a sloping, elongated shell that looks somewhat like a stretched-out pyramid.

The debris shelter's doorway is also a triangle, sited on one side of the shelter's highest end. I typically use the supporting live tree as one side of the doorway, then build the wall on that side toward it until the right-triangle entrance is just large enough to crawl through. The wall on the opposite side of the tree should be completely enclosed up to the tree trunk.

Although it might look solid from the outside, you'll see by crawling inside that there are perhaps hundreds of gaps through which you can see daylight, all of them potential entry points for rain and wind. Draping the shelter with a waterproof sheet held in place by heavy sticks leaned against the walls rectifies this problem, but wet leaves from the forest floor, grasses and mud, or even wads of green bracken ferns can also be used to plug the holes. You'll need to crawl into and out of the shelter a few times to inspect for cracks of daylight, but in most forests even a first-time builder should find his debris hut finished to this point in about an hour.

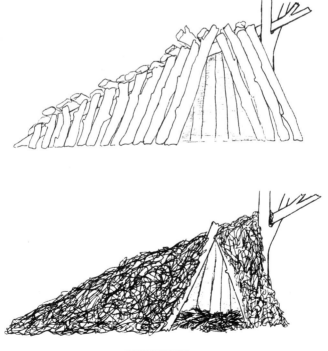

DEBRIS HUT

Because a debris shelter must always be unheated due to the real flammability of its construction materials, it must have a bed, or sleeping pallet (described later on page 170) inside to prevent your body heat from being sucked into the ground. Building the shelter just large enough to contain its occupant helps retain body heat in cold weather, much like an oversize sleeping bag. The entrance can be sealed by leaning heavy branches against its outer wall from the inside.

Shingle Hut

This variation on the debris hut gets its name from the overlapping "shingles" that are layered over its frame. Logs and stumps generally decay from the inside, leaving a hard wooden outer shell. Splitting apart this shell with a machete or hatchet (or just by stomping it) results in two or more—depending on the diameter of the shell—convex lengths of wood that look something like the clay tiles used in Spanish haciendas.

Like shingles, these split-off lengths can be laid curved-side up onto the skeleton frame of a debris hut fitted to allow as little gap as possible between, and held in place by their own cumulative weight. Begin with a row of shingles across the bottom of the shelter, than add another row of overlapping shingles just above them, then another just above that until the apex of the roof is covered. Some fitting and wedging will be required, and if materials are available it doesn't hurt to add a second layer of shingles. Like the debris shelter, its doorway can be closed to the elements, sometimes with just one or two large shingles. The end result is a very strong shell that can be made entirely rainproof and capable of withstanding the weight of a heavy snowfall.

Earth Shelter

The earth, or dugout, shelter, is the domicile I most recommend for long-term use—for instance, if you've survived a light-plane crash on the wrong side of a mountain range with winter coming on hard. Although I generally opt for going home in a real survival circumstance, there are any number of situations in which a survivalist might be stranded in the wilderness for an extended time. An earth shelter requires some effort to create, de-

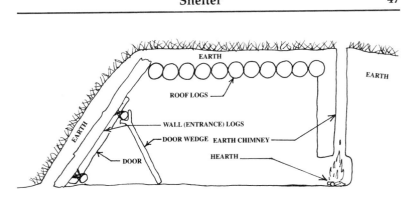

EARTH DUGOUT

The earth dugout begins as a hole dug into the side of a hill. After a roof and front wall have been constructed of logs covered with dirt, and a door has been fashioned, the dugout becomes a four-season shelter that can be used indefinitely if need be.

pending on how large you want your quarters to be, but it's warm in the cold, cool in the heat, and might be better called a house than a shelter.

As the name implies, an earth shelter is comprised primarily of earth, so this is not a shelter suitable for swamps and lowland places where digging more than a few inches will strike water. The best and easiest sites are usually on higher ground with good drainage and incorporate a natural knoll or small ridge into their design. Excavating a trench inward through the face of such a knoll (all the way through if you want a back door) creates a hole that will serve as your living quarters for as long as you need, so make it large enough to be comfortable.

Most regions, whether desert, woods, or jungle, will offer resistance to excavation in the form of tough roots and large rocks. A folding shovel makes the excavation process much easier, but the Ontario Knife SP8 survival machete is nearly its equal for this task. A good survival knife will also do in a pinch, and if you've no tools at all—which I like to believe could never happen—a slab of wood split from the outside of a rotting stump or log works well enough.

Once you've excavated a hole large enough to call home, the next step is to put a roof over it. Dead logs and branches long enough to span the top of the hole are placed across it, all of them parallel to one another, until no daylight can be seen through the roof from below.

If possible, the next layer to go onto your dugout's roof should be waterproof, or at least dirtproof. A sheet of verathane or a Space Blanket works well, but in forested places you can make do with leafy humus stuffed into the cracks between members of the base roof.

The last layer to go onto your dugout's roof is the soil from its excavation. Kept from falling through by the dense roof below, this foot-thick earthen roof is too deep for frost to penetrate except on the coldest of winter days. A layer of leaves or ferns laid atop the dirt and weighted by deadwood further keeps out rain and prevents loose soil from washing away.

Closing the front of the shelter is accomplished by leaning large, long pieces of wood side by side against the entrance from either side, leaving only a body-size opening in their center. Packing wet leaves, grass and mud, or sod into the cracks between helps seal out the elements. In cold weather the shelter's small doorway can be sealed from the outside entirely with a groundsheet draped over it and weighted with a log or rock. I've also woven doors from interlaced springy green branches (willow, dogwood, cedar), but I recommend propping these in place from the inside in places where snowfall is heavy.

One of an earth shelter's better points is that it can be heated from the inside by what might best be described as a small fireplace. Being dirt, the walls are of course fireproof, so you can excavate a 2-foot-diameter hole into one wall and vent it to the sky through a narrow (about 10-inch-diameter) chimney hole dug down to it from above. The fire pit itself should be excavated to a depth of at least 6 inches to prevent hot coals from popping out onto you. Laying a small fire in this makeshift fireplace will heat the closed shelter to shirtsleeve temperatures even in a subzero blow.

Snow Dugout

This winter shelter makes use of deep hardpack snow to provide shelter, like the classic snow trench and snow cave shelters, except in this case you needn't burn off a day's calories during the excavation process.

At least 4 feet of hardpack (compressed) snow on the ground is a prerequisite to the snow dugout's construction. I start with a large, crackling fire, as hot as I can build it, and keep it well fueled

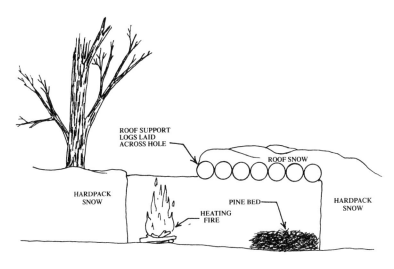

ROOF SUPPORT
LOGS LAID
ACROSS HOLE

ROOF SNOW

HARDPACK
SNOW

PINE BED

HARDPACK
SNOW

HEATING
FIRE

SNOW DUGOUT

until it has burned a hole through the snow and down to bare earth. When the hole has reached a diameter large enough to accommodate my prone body at its bottom (about 7 feet), I kick the fire to one end and rebuild it to a smaller, more usable size.

I cover the end of the hole opposite the fire with a platform of deadwood laid side by side across the rim of the hole, just like the roof described above under "Earth Shelter," except that in this case half the hole is left uncovered to let smoke escape. A sleeping pallet under the roof keeps falling snow off the sleeper and prevents body heat from absorbing into the ground. A small fire at the opposite end of the hole radiates heat that is reflected onto the sleeper from all sides by the dugout's walls, and at the same time repels falling snow with waves of heat rising from below.

SLEEPING WARM

A good shelter negates the effects of rain and wind, and helps retain lost body heat, but nighttime temperatures of 50 degrees F or below demand a little more insulation. Following are several tricks that veteran outdoorsmen employ to keep warm and get a good night's sleep in cold weather.

The Essential Bed

No hardship you might face in a real-world survival scenario will have more impact on your health and safety than the ability to get a good night's sleep. Rest is essential to good health, and beating down your own immune system through exhaustion or any other hardship is never conducive to survival.

The biggest problem is cold. Few places on earth don't get cold enough to induce hypothermia at least some of the time, so retaining body heat at a level comfortable enough to allow sound, preferably undisturbed, sleep is of primary importance.

Sleeping Pads

The First Law of Thermodynamics states that heat always travels to cold, so unless the earth you're sleeping on maintains a constant temperature of at least 70 degrees F all night, you'll need an insulated bed to prevent direct contact with the ground. In warmer climates and seasons, a good sleeping bag is sufficient by itself, but if the earth is cooling in autumn, or still warming up in spring, it can easily absorb enough body heat to cause hypothermia and prevent sound sleep.

Closed-cell foam sleeping pads, such as the Slumberjack R3 model or Cascade Designs Link Rest (both $12), are my first choice as a bed on cold ground. I often use mine for ambushing wild animals with camera or gun because the pad allows me to lie prone for long hours on cold ground, rock, snow, and sometimes atop the ice of a frozen lake. In winter I consider a closed-cell foam pad to be a must-have survival tool.

Sleeping Pallets

But sleeping pads are a relatively new innovation, and when I was a boy, making deer camp or spending the night on a trapline meant first laying a sleeping pallet. This is simply a platform of fairly straight body-length branches or dead logs laid side by side on the ground to form a pallet wide enough to accommodate your body. This pallet is the vital insulating layer between your body and ground, and is effective even on ice or snow. Grasses, ferns, pine boughs, or whatever natural padding materials are available help

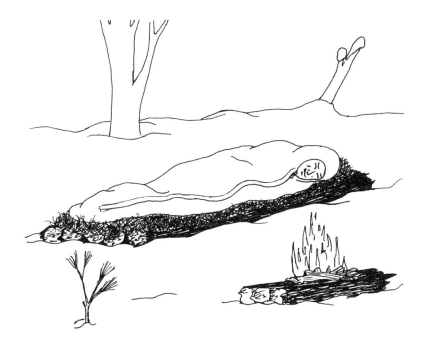

A sleeping pallet is essential for sleeping
warm on cold ground.

soften bumps and protrusions, and if necessary you can pitch a tent
or bivy, or build a shelter, atop the completed pallet.

Bedrolls

The best survival bedroll is a good, synthetic-fill sleeping bag
that will dry quickly and retain most of its warmth even when wet
(see chapter 1). Because such a sleeping bag didn't exist when I was
boy, for many years I slept soundly rolled into a six-point woolen
Indian blanket. Only a hard rain could penetrate the thick wool,
which even then retained most of my body heat, and many morn-
ings I awoke after a restful sleep to find myself buried under several
inches of fresh snow. The blanket's only downside was its weight,
which ran about 7 pounds.

Another good emergency bedroll that is probably more common in most homes than a woolen blanket is a synthetic blanket of acrylic or other plastic fibers. This blanket is probably most often seen between a top sheet and bedspread, but with a weight of under 2 pounds and the same ability to retain heat when wet, these also make pretty fair emergency bedrolls. Two blankets can be doubled for increased protection in colder weather, but a single blanket inside a shelter and atop a good bed will keep an average sleeper warm down to 40 degrees F.

In a pinch almost any blanket-size piece of fabric can serve as a bedroll. In this instance it doesn't really matter what material the blanket is made from, because its insulating value will be provided by natural materials taken from the surrounding environment. Plastic tarpaulins are great, but even a linen bedsheet will suffice, because this bed relies on a groundsheet only to hold its insulation in place, much like the shell of a sleeping bag.

Beginning with a good sleeping pallet, pile its surface high with dry leaves, ferns, and whatever foliage is available. Climb into the center of this pile of dry, airy insulation and lie down. Beginning at your feet, pile the insulating foliage atop your body, covering it with the groundsheet as you work upward toward your head. Held in place by the sheet, the insulating layer, which should have a consistent thickness of 6 inches or more over your whole body, will retain body heat surprisingly well down to subfreezing temps.

Another trick that a rail-riding fellow I once knew claimed saved his life is burying your entire body under a foot or so of sand or gravel. This fellow was hitching on a freight train through a remote stretch of Nevada desert when the empty car he was riding in was pushed onto a side rail and left behind. Faced with temperatures well below freezing after sunset and no more trains until morning, the man buried his body under the rocky sand, his face covered by a shirt, and slept soundly till morning. I've tried this method in the beach sand of Lake Michigan's shoreline in temperatures down to 40 degrees F, and it seems like a pretty good last-ditch resort on a cold night. The tricks are to make certain that the soil you use is dry—because wet soil sucks heat from your body—and to line its bottom with whatever dry foliage is available.

Water

In humans death from dehydration occurs after roughly 72 hours of deprivation, and for the last day a victim will likely be weak and incoherent, or even unconscious. No human survives long without water.

With three-quarters of our home planet submerged, you might think that getting a drink would be easy, but the human body is a sensitive and finicky piece of biomachinery. That most of the water on earth is undrinkable salt water tells me God has a sense of humor, but freshwater lakes, rivers, and even the clearest mountain streams can also harbor dangerous pathogens. Adding to these natural problems are man-made poisons such as fertilizer, pesticides, and herbicides that run into waterways from golf courses and farmland.

HOW MUCH WATER DO I NEED?

Most experts recommend that an average adult male consume 1 gallon of water per day. In real life an individual's actual daily needs tend to vary downward from there, depending on body size, fitness and exertion levels, and ambient temperatures, but a gallon a day is a safe benchmark.

However much water an individual requires under a given set of conditions, the importance of keeping well hydrated cannot be overstated. The role water plays in our bodies is essentially that of an irrigant, flushing dead and depleted matter from the organs. Dehydration slows down this cleansing process, resulting in higher levels of biological toxins within the body. This in turn places a real strain on the immune system, compromising the body's ability to resist infectious microorganisms.

The first and most obvious symptom of dehydration is a darkening of the urine. Kidneys that are well flushed produce urine that is pale yellow or even clear; darker hues indicate higher concentrations of toxins. If your urine seems darker than normal, take this as a warning to drink more water.

The next most likely affliction caused by dehydration is constipation, which is nearly always attributable to not drinking enough water. Lacking sufficient moisture, excreta in the colon become dry and hard, and may form a painful blockage that can itself have serious, even fatal consequences.

Being a coffee addict has kept me from having this particular problem, but I recall a winter camping companion who once became so constipated from simple dehydration that he actually had to remove the hard, ball-shaped feces from his colon with a finger. The same problem, with the same unattractive remedy, is described in *Alive*, Piers Paul Read's book about a Paraguayan soccer team whose plane went down in the Cordillera mountain range separating Chile and Argentina in 1973.

Water is also a vital part of the body's cooling system. If temperatures or exertion levels are high enough to cause heavy perspiration, loss of body water must be countered by drinking more fluids. Under very warm conditions, perspiration loss can exceed a pint an hour, and the effect can be compared to a car with a leaky cooling system: Less coolant means higher operating temperatures than individual components are meant to handle, and unless more fluid is added, both human and machine will cease to operate.

Dehydration can also occur in cold temperatures. Layered clothing can absorb a large amount of perspiration unnoticed, and victims seldom feel overheated or even thirsty. Again, urine color is probably the most important indication that you aren't drinking enough, but in this case you're also likely to feel chilled, because the body uses water to distribute heat.

THE DANGERS OF DRINKING UNTREATED WATER

The image of a buckskin-clad Indian cupping water to his mouth from a crystal stream is one we've all seen. Unfortunately, the romantic inference that natural waters have ever been safe to drink is incorrect. Drinking directly from any stream or pool is just asking for trouble.

The biggest danger comes from runoff. Rain and melting snows wash ground contaminants into nearby bodies of water, where animals and, to an alarming degree these days, humans ingest them through drinking. Farms and golf courses are serious contributors, and the recent overpopulation of flesh-eating *Pfisteria* microbes in North Carolina has been directly linked to fertilizer runoff from both.

Aquatic parasites pose the most immediate threat to humans. A good deal about aquatic parasites remains unknown to this day, but we do know they typically exist in water as viable eggs or free-swimming larvae. Many are species-specific, meaning that an intestinal parasite common to dogs may be entirely harmless to humans and cats. Several occupy intermediate hosts, such as fish, crayfish, and aquatic snails, whose flesh and feces can infect humans with the next stage of a parasite.

Once ingested, the eggs or larvae are immediately set upon by their intended victim's immune system. If the intruders' numbers are low enough, or if the victim has developed immunity from prior exposure to a similar parasite, the immune system will likely kill all invaders before they can get a foothold: one more good argument for a full belly and a good night's sleep.

But if the parasitic organisms overwhelm the body's defenses, and one or more of them manages to attach itself to the intestinal wall or stomach, it becomes invulnerable to the victim's autoimmune system. Adding to this problem is the possibility that several types of parasitic organisms might be ingested from a single untreated drink.

Pathogens found in the natural waters of North America are typically limited to intestinal parasites of the flagellate family, such as *Giardia, Cryptosporidium,* and *Cyclospora.* But *Paragonimus,* a lung fluke native to Asia and the East Indies, may have already become established in Florida, and there are numerous other parasitic worms, or flukes, that should be guarded against. Fortunately, all are rendered harmless by the same sterilization and filtration methods.

Once attached to a target organ within the victim's body, a parasite begins to develop, drawing nourishment from the affected organ. Within a week—sometimes as little as two days—victims begin to experience nausea, bouts of diarrhea mixed with periods of constipation, and fever with an influenzalike achiness.

For most species of parasite, growth to maturity takes about two months, during which victims suffer a mild form of malnutrition because invaders are literally stealing their food before it can be absorbed by the intestines. Some, like *Cryptosporidium*, coat victims' intestines with a mucuslike secretion that hinders their ability to metabolize food. When the bisexual invaders mature, they lay hundreds to thousands of eggs per adult, die, and are then expelled with their eggs in the feces of their victims. Rain and melting snow help wash the living eggs into a nearby waterway, where the entire symbiotic process begins anew.

Parasitic organisms are not designed by nature to be fatal to their hosts, because that would be counterproductive to their own survival. Deaths have resulted, however, because most Americans have had little or no exposure to aquatic parasites, and the full brunt of their attack is more than some immune systems can handle. Diabetics are especially at risk, but anyone with a preexisting medical problem that already places a strain on his body's resources should take pains to avoid all parasites.

Bacterial infections such as typhoid and cholera aren't of much concern in nature, but in civilization, where large numbers of people generate large amounts of sewage and garbage, these often-fatal diseases still occur. I was in Grand Rapids, Michigan's second largest city, in 1982 when cholera was found in the city's tap water after a filter at the municipal sewage treatment plant malfunctioned. Fortunately, most waterborne bacterial infections still respond to antibiotics, although a few, like tuberculosis, are becoming not only prevalent in nature but resistant to drugs as well.

Viruses dangerous to humans are almost never encountered in nature, but once again they could be a problem in a communal setting. Hepatitis, meningitis, and herpes are among the more common viral infections found in third-world villages, refugee camps, and other densely occupied places where proper waste treatment is lacking. Unlike bacteria, viruses are usually fragile and unable to survive outside a host for more than a few minutes, so transmission typically occurs not from water, but from contact with a person already infected.

Chemical toxins in our drinking water pose an almost universal health hazard these days. From heavy metals in tap water to the scum of petroleum floating at every marina to runoff from farms and golf courses, there are many nonbiological reasons to be cautious about the water we drink. Most waterborne chemical toxins are insidious, collecting in their victims' tissues for weeks or even years before causing serious illness.

The exception is the desert, where natural water holes are notorious for being poisoned with alkalai from the earth, and sometimes from the carcasses of animals unlucky enough to discover this fact the hard way. Windmill-pumped wells scattered throughout the desert provide water that is safe for consumption, but any natural water hole is suspect.

MAKING WATER POTABLE

American history is peppered with epidemics of waterborne ailments that once wiped out whole settlements and stopped wagon trains in their tracks with sometimes-fatal dysentery. Migrants heading westward were most likely the victims of a common parasitic flagellate such as *Giardia*. Armed with the information provided by computer-age science, a modern survivalist is far less likely to become a victim of waterborne ailments.

Chemical Water Treatments

Iodine is the best-known chemical water treatment, and for many years it was thought to be a complete defense against all types of aquatic parasites. That's why I was perplexed when a companion contracted *Cryptosporidium* during a backpacking trip to Michigan's Hiawatha National Forest in 1996. A few months later it was discovered that *Cryptosporidium* is not completely killed by iodine. At about the same time, microbiologists introduced us to a previously unknown pathogenic flagellate called *Cyclospora*, which is also resistant to iodine.

Iodine is still believed to kill *Giardia lamblia* and all viruses and bacteria, however, so I still include it in my water-treatment kit. Iodine tablets are available for about $6 per bottle of 100, but my experience has been that these tend to be reduced to powder by the rigors of cross-country travel. Tincture of iodine (liquid) in a concentration of three drops per quart (maximum) is just as effective, but it's more durable in a survival kit and priced at less than $1 in most pharmacies and department stores. Mix the iodized water well by shaking the canteen, slashing some over its mouth; wait 15 minutes before drinking.

Chlorine also kills viruses and bacteria, but not *Giardia, Cryptosporidium, Cyclospora,* or parasitic flatworms (flukes). This heretofore-unknown fact was made obvious during the war in Vietnam, when American soldiers were issued chlorine-based Halozone tablets that were supposed to kill the many flagellates and flukes found in that region's waters. They didn't, and probably most combat soldiers contracted severe parasitic dysentery at some point during their tours of duty.

Boiling

Boiling is the oldest form of water purification, and it remains one of the most effective even today. No harmful organism yet discovered can survive being boiled. In fact, most harmful organisms die at 180 degrees F, the temperature of hot tap water.

Fresh water reaches a rolling boil when heated to a temperature of 212 degrees F (100 degrees Celsius) at sea level, under a nominal atmospheric pressure of 14.7 pounds per square inch (psi). Simply heating water to a rolling boil is more than sufficient to make it potable; there is no need to evaporate away valuable drinking water by boiling it for 15 or 20 minutes.

An exception to this rule occurs at elevations above 3,000 feet. In mountain country, where thinning air and decreased atmospheric pressure can cause water to reach a hard boil at temperatures just above lukewarm, heating vessels must be covered, and even weighted down with a rock. Without a lid to contain and pressurize the water inside, it can simply evaporate away without ever becoming hot enough to kill all the pathogenic critters within.

If your source of water is a clear-looking stream or lake, the water you draw can be boiled and drunk as is after cooling. In fact, I

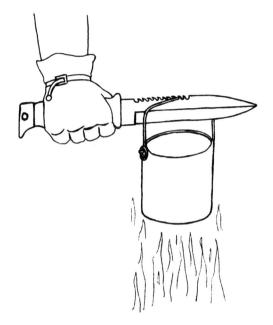

USING A SURVIVAL KNIFE AND
LEATHER GLOVES TO LIFT A POT OF
BOILED WATER FROM A CAMPFIRE

generally prefer boiled water because, unlike filtering, none of a water's natural minerals are removed or affected by the process. We now know that minerals are essential to the proper absorption of some vitamins, and boiled, unfiltered water is a good source of necessary electrolytes.

Too many minerals can be a problem, however, when they take the form of suspended mud or silt. Boiling will make the murkiest water safe to drink where parasites are concerned, but attempting to drink gritty water is almost guaranteed to trigger your gag reflex. It does no good to eat or drink anything you can't keep in your stomach.

The problem of grit and sediment is most easily solved by first pouring water intended for boiling through a handkerchief or similar cloth. Straining through cloth will not remove microscopic parasites or germs, but it will remove mosquito larvae and other "wigglers" as well as the coarsest sediment and mud.

Condensation Stills

Condensation stills have been in use for decades, since modern manufactured plastics and other materials made them feasible to construct and use. A condensation still works by evaporating water in a closed container where the liquid element is separated by heat into its two component gases, hydrogen and oxygen. Both these gases then rise to the top of the containment vessel, leaving heavier contaminants behind, and condense back into drinkable distilled water.

Solar Still: This is the condensation still most recommended in survival manuals, and manufactured versions of the device have long been standard equipment for naval life rafts. The land survivalst's version most often consists of a hole excavated in moist soil and covered with clear plastic, or verathane, sheeting. The waterproof sheet is held in place and sealed over the hole by pegs or weights placed around its perimeter. A stone placed in the center of the sheet causes it to sag in the middle, forming a sort of funnel that channels recondensed distilled water into a cup placed at the bottom of the hole directly below. Water or even crushed vegetation dumped into the bottom of the hole is heated by sunlight passing through the verathane. The sun's warmth evaporates whatever wa-

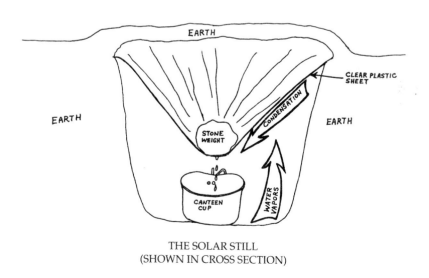

THE SOLAR STILL
(SHOWN IN CROSS SECTION)

ter is present in the hole into vapors that condense and collect as water droplets against the plastic roof. Any liquid that contains water can be used in this distillation process, including urine and engine coolant.

The biggest problem is that solar stills are not very efficient, especially in places where relative humidity keeps the air more or less saturated with moisture, because they rely solely on the sun for evaporation. For this reason, only clear plastic sheeting that allows sunlight to pass through freely from above should be used, and the edges of the sheet should be well sealed around its perimeter to prevent water vapors from escaping under its edges.

Heated Condensation Still: This type of condensation still is the best choice for survival situations involving several people, or even more. Because it relies on heat not from the sun but from a hot wood fire below, it can be kept in operation 24 hours a day if necessary. Like the solar condensation still, it can separate potable water from agricultural runoff, seawater, or engine coolant.

Construction of a heated condensation still is simple, and many backcountry drivers already carry the means in their vehicles. A clean metal gasoline can works very well as a heating vessel. A rubber hose fitted tightly into the fill cap (already a feature on

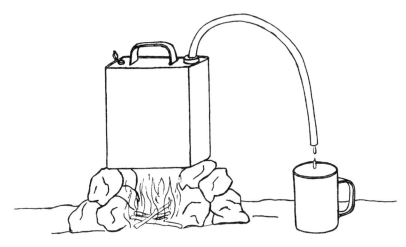

A HEATED CONDENSATION STILL CAN
BE FASHIONED FROM A CLEAN GASOLINE
CAN AND RUBBER HOSE

many gas cans) acts to channel steam vapors to the outside, where they cool and recondense into water that drips from its end.

For the sake of convenience, fires placed under a heated condensation still should be kept just large enough to heat the can's bottom. There's no chance that the can will explode, because any excess steam pressure is simply vented off as water.

FINDING WATER

As an old desert trekker like the late Edward Abbey would be quick to point out, it doesn't do much good to have drinking-water outfit if you can't find water. Fortunately, the earth is mostly water, and there are few places where you can't find enough to drink within a day's walk. Maps made for desert hiking include the locations of watering holes, some of which are drilled wells pumped by windmills that can be seen from several miles across open desert. In less arid terrain water is usually more plentiful and easier to find, but you still need to know the best places to look.

Natural Springs

Springs are a woodsman's best source of natural water. A spring is essentially a leak in the water table, a place where cold water below ground is squeezed through many tons of earth to gush from lowland hillsides. Occasionally water is diverted upward by the same pressure—again, usually in lowland areas—to become a natural fountain, or artesian well.

I've heard rumors that not all artesian wells are to be trusted, but no one I know who has drunk from a springhead flowing out of a hillside has ever gotten anything but a good drink. This margin of safety extends only to springheads; many springs turn into creeks, which then merge into rivers. The farther downstream you get from a "feeder" spring, the greater the possibility of contamination from fecal and chemical runoff.

I'd also be wary of any water flowing away from farmlands and golf courses, both of which use large amounts of pesticides and herbicides that are leached or washed by rain and snowmelt into groundwater. Boiling will not remove chemical contaminants, and even springwater drawn from agricultural areas should be filtered or distilled.

If circumstances dictate that you drink directly from a spring-head you've judged safe, never simply fall onto your belly and suck up cold water the way movie actors do. If you're very hot and thirsty, a sudden shot of cold water to the stomach can literally knock you out, and lying unconscious facedown in a pool of water won't help your chances of survival. Instead, use a drinking vessel or your cupped hand to bring the water to your lips. A plastic or rubber hose, like the uncontaminated output hose from a water filter, works well as a straw that lets a thirsty hiker drink from spring-heads without actually reaching the water.

Seepage Wells

Seepage wells date back to biblical times. Probably most folks today know them as wishing wells and lawn ornaments, but seepage wells were once found in every village around the world, and in desert regions they were often the sole reason for a community's existence. Village wells of old were usually well looked after, protected from contamination by a stone wall around the perimeter and sometimes by a roof to keep out bird droppings.

A seepage well is really nothing more complicated than a hole dug downward until its bottom fills with water, ideally in a location where there is as little earth between the water table and the person digging as possible. After you allow the sediment to settle, water taken from the hole may be drawn for drinking or cooking. I'd still avoid agricultural and other areas where groundwater is suspect, but I've often dug shallow seepage wells next to rivers and lakes whose waters I would never drink from directly.

Dry water holes can also be revived with a seepage well, a trick known by Indians of the desert southwest. Flowing springs and open pools that appear dried up are nearly always still there, just not with enough flow or volume to flood onto the surface. Again, the most likely spots are in lowland areas, sometimes in a rock basin, where a few inches to a few feet of soil protect the remaining liquid from evaporation. If you encounter dampness after digging a foot or so into dry sand or soil, the spot is a likely candidate for a seepage well.

Rainwater

I'd like to say that rainwater is always safe to drink, as it has been throughout history, but in this era of acid rain I doubt that this still holds true within many miles of smog-producing cities like Los Angeles, Dayton, or Detroit. Still, rainwater has proven a valuable source of drinking water since the time when every cabin had a rain barrel. When U.S. Air Force Lieutenant Colonel Iceal Hambleton was shot down over North Vietnam in 1972, he used the rubberized map from his survival vest to collect rainwater while successfully eluding pursuers who dearly wanted to ask him about his specialty in electronic warfare.

The trick to collecting rain for drinking is to gather as many drops as possible and channel them to a reservoir. A 5- by 8-foot sheet of plastic (verathane) tied horizontally between trees a few inches above the ground and weighted with a rock in its center can produce a gallon of drinking water a day in a drizzling rain. Foil-laminated Space Blankets are equally efficient, as is the ultralight tarp from Integral Designs that I carry in my own survival kit. The beauty of any of these is that you can quickly string one up as a lean-to roof between trees and take shelter below while rainwater rolling off the top is channeled directly into a canteen.

In rock country you can expect to find pools of collected rainwater in stone basins several days after the last precipitation. These sometimes look clean, especially after a rainfall, but that same shower probably washed in bird guano and animal scat that contain parasites. I don't advise drinking water from these natural catch basins without first filtering or boiling.

Collecting Dew

Dewfall is a phenomenon that occurs every evening when warmed airborne moisture vapors rapidly cool after the sun's disappearance over the horizon. Depending on temperature and humidity, the amount of drinkable dew collected by a 5- by 8-foot tarpaulin can exceed a pint per night.

Absorbent cloths (cotton) and especially ordinary square sponges can be used to more actively gather fallen dew. A sponge pressed onto dew-wet grasses, rocks, and other foliage will become saturated with several times its own weight in water, which can then be squeezed into a container.

TRANSPORTING WATER

Anyone who spends even a few hours in the wilderness should consider a canteen of water required equipment. In a genuine survival situation it's never a good plan to walk from one water hole to another, and without a water container it can be difficult or even impossible to make unsafe water fit for consumption.

Makeshift Canteens

As I've discovered from camping in mountain country where the nearest water is 500 feet down a steep granite grade, there can come a time when you'll want to carry more water than the canteens in your survival kit can hold. And of course there are also those occasional survival situations where you need a canteen to transport water but don't have one.

The classic survivalist's water carrier is a deer intestine tightly knotted at the bottom and closed with a looser slipknot at the top. Excellent idea if you can find a couple of feet of deer intestine lying around, but I generally find that there are numerous other more readily available means for taking more water with you when you leave.

Plastic soda-pop and sports-drink bottles are almost ubiquitous today, even on remote hiking trails where I keep picking them up, and these will hold drinking water as well as they held their original contents. Plastic bottles that did not originally hold a beverage or nontoxic liquid should never be used, but probably most drivers I know have an empty pop bottle rolling around somewhere in their cars.

Waterproof breathable socks have become a permanent fixture in all my backpacks, because they turn even sandals into waterproof footwear, and because they make good booties for midnight trips to the camp pee tree. They also make pretty fair emergency canteens when turned inside out, filled with potable water, and tied shut at their tops with a piece of cord.

The bag-and-rag canteen is a last-ditch emergency water carrier that motorists can make from the trash that seems to accumulate in everyone's vehicle. Empty plastic and Mylar bags that held potato chips or other snacks aren't strong or watertight enough to hold water by themselves, but they can contain water-soaked cotton rags or sponges placed inside. A large potato chip bag filled with saturated towels or clothing, then tied shut, can contain a quart of water for days, ready to be squeezed out when you need it.

STORING WATER

In recent times the science of storing water for drinking and cooking has become a topic of conversation among folks who have seen from the misfortunes of others that utilities can go off-line for extended periods. If you're entirely dependent on a public utility for your drinking water, it doesn't hurt to have at least three days' worth of potable water on hand for drinking and cooking. Considering the impact a water utility shutdown could have in an urban environment, I think having a supply of water in reserve for everyone in a household (including pets, of course) is more prudence than paranoia.

Because it's unlikely that any American town would suffer a loss of water for more than three days before someone began trucking the stuff in, figure on this amount of time and water as a minimum. A good rule of thumb is 1 gallon of drinking water per person per day. Next come 2 gallons a day for cooking, followed, if possible, by 4 or more gallons a day for toilet flushing.

Suitable containers for long-term water storage do not include milk jugs. Because milk has a short shelf life, it can be packaged in a biodegradable plastic made to decay rapidly by the addition of cornstarch, which means that any liquid stored in a milk jug can be counted on to leak out in a month or so.

Soda-pop bottles work great for storing water, as do chlorine bleach jugs and screw-top vegetable or fruit juice bottles. Better yet is a 5-gallon plastic jerry can—but never drink from or store water in any plastic container whose original contents wouldn't be safe for human consumption. Despite appearances, plastics are porous and can absorb toxic or caustic chemicals, which explains the DO NOT REUSE BOTTLE warning many carry on their labels.

One mostly unwarranted concern about storing water for an unforeseen emergency is keeping the liquid drinkable. In fact, water from local utilities is already filtered and chlorinated to reduce the danger from viruses, bacteria, and parasitic organisms to zero (barring glitches at the treatment plant). The bottom line is that city water may be stored indefinitely with no further treatment.

Most authorities recommend that stored water, treated or otherwise, be kept in a cool, dark place to retard the possible growth of algae. Water can get a stale taste after many months of storage, but I haven't suffered ill effects from drinking old water. Suspicious water can be boiled or filtered, making it potable even if it has been contaminated.

5

Medicine

My breath condensed before me in thin white vapors as I knelt atop the snow, hacking wedge-shaped pieces of meat from a solidly frozen whitetail neck with my Buck M9 field knife. The venison was bait for drawing in a pack of gray wolves that had recently migrated to Michigan's Lower Peninsula. The notches around its perimeter were needed to securely hold the rope to which it would be tied, suspended from a half-downed spruce.

I was nearly finished when the Buck's heavy 6 ¾-inch blade skipped off the frozen meat and slammed hard, edge-first, into the index finger of my opposite hand, which had been holding the neck. Air hissed through my clenched teeth as well-honed steel chopped deep into my first knuckle. I immediately pressed hard against the wound with a thumb to stanch the blood flowing from it, but the finger of my woolen glove liner was sliced neatly halfway through, and I knew this was a bad one.

With my good hand, I quickly hoisted and tied off the venison, then headed for camp—and my first-aid kit—nearly 2 miles away. Because this wasn't the first time I'd done potentially serious harm to myself in the woods with a bonehead stunt, I anticipated the shock-generated nausea, chills, and sweating that always accompany bone-deep injuries. Knowing what to expect didn't make enduring it more pleasant, however.

At camp I slipped the first-aid kit from its pocket in my back-pack with my free hand, never releasing the pressure against the wound as I took out a roll of self-adhesive safety, or finger, tape and a single-application packet of antibiotic ointment. With these items at the ready, I stripped off the slashed glove liner in one quick motion. Bright blood spurted outward as soon as the pressure was released, but before the gash was obscured I was able to confirm visually that muscle, bone, and cartilage had been deeply damaged.

My first concern was to stop the bleeding as quickly as possible. With sunset the mercury had already dropped to –7 degrees F, and it was falling fast toward an overnight low of –16 under a clear, moonlit sky. I was alone, 10 miles from civilization, and I wasn't scheduled to be picked up for another three days. It wasn't an optimal time or place to be leaking important body fluids.

I wrapped the injured finger with several snug turns of safety tape, gently squeezing both sides of the cut together and stanching the flow of blood completely—much like taping a ruptured automobile radiator hose. It throbbed a bit that night, but by morning the gash had closed sufficiently to be washed in a nearby spring, sterilized, then rebandaged with no further blood loss.

I'll always have a long crescent-shaped scar from that experience to remind me of what can happen to a woodsman who forgets his place for even a moment, but it could have been a lot worse. The injury might easily have been more severe, even an amputation, and I could have been much farther from base camp. Too, gangrene is a real concern in temperatures cold enough to kill exposed skin; more than a few old-timers lost parts of their anatomy—or their lives—proving this.

Worst of all, I might not have had the advantages of a well-provisioned and practical first-aid kit, and that could have made a bad situation intolerable. With it, a wound serious enough to make sensible folks in civilization seek medical attention had quickly been reduced to a relatively minor inconvenience under conditions that did not favor the injured. Without it, the situation would certainly have been more challenging.

I'd really like to suggest a ready-made medical kit for back-packing, but none has yet proven functional enough to merit a recommendation. That needn't be a bad thing, however, because assembling your own field first-aid kit usually results in a compact no-fluff unit that's lighter, less expensive, and specifically tailored to the environment in which it will be used.

I cannot offer medical advice, so the following remedies are given only as examples of the items you'd find in my own first-aid kits. I will say that each of these components has earned its place over the years, with the end result being a functionally sleek medical kit that can treat most injuries quicky and efficiently.

SKIN LACERATIONS

The most common type of injury in the woods is a cut or scrape to the fingers or hands. Most occur from slips while using cutting instruments such as knife, hatchet, or camp saw, with the remainder coming from encounters with sharp sticks, falls on rock, and assorted missteps.

Only two items are needed to address the majority of skin punctures and cuts a camper might suffer: A roll of 1-inch-wide safety tape and a small tube of nonprescription triple-antibiotic ointment (Neosporin or its equivalent). The latter prevents contamination and infection of the wound, while the former has so many uses that I consider it a fundamental component of every medical kit.

Cotton-gauze safety tape is unique in that it sticks tenaciously to itself but nothing else, which makes it especially useful for binding wounds, wrapping splints in place, or immobilizing the head of someone with a suspected spinal injury. A few snug (not tight) wraps will stop bleeding by literally sealing off a wound, without the painful, often injurious constrictive pressure of a conventional tourniquet, and the tape won't bond to damaged tissue. Infectious contaminants are sealed out while the wound knits back together, and unlike most bandages, safety tape remains in place when wet.

Safety tape can also help prevent accidents by providing a no-slip wrapped grip for knife, ax, and tool handles. A variety of colors is available, with standard widths ranging from ½ inch to 3 inches. A free sample roll of this useful multipurpose tape can be obtained by calling General Bandages, Inc., at 1 (800) 922–1422.

For lacerations on the scalp, abdomen, or other places where squeezing a wound's edges together with safety tape isn't feasible, I carry butterfly sutures, namely Steri-Strips. These very sticky peel-and-press tapes can be found at most pharmacies, and are the next best thing to stitches for closing open, even bleeding wounds.

I feel obligated to insert a caveat at this point: Never, ever attempt to stitch shut an open wound with needle and thread, à la Rambo. I know a fellow who came too close to losing his entire leg to gangrene after sewing up a relatively minor gash in his thigh. The reason doctors tend to avoid using stitches these days is because piercing the already-damaged skin of a wound increases pain and swelling, and greatly increases the possibility of introducing infectious contaminants, which are then sealed in.

MEDICINES

Painkillers

Analgesics, or painkillers, are a must-have component of any field first-aid kit. A sprained ankle, jammed thumb, earache, or toothache can make any camping trip unpleasant, if not downright unbearable. Even minor injuries tend to throb painfully, especially at night, and they can rob you of the sleep needed to keep your body's immune system strong.

Ibuprofen, best known by its prescription-strength name, Motrin, was made legal for over-the-counter sale a decade ago, and its value to an injured woodsman is hard to exaggerate. Each nonprescription-strength 200-milligram tablet delivers the same painkilling power as two acetaminophen (Tylenol) tablets, but unlike acetaminophen or aspirin, ibuprofen can be "stacked" to increase its potency. Up to four tablets can be safely ingested in a single dose (the equivalent of one 800-milligram Motrin dose) to quadruple the drug's analgesic strength. Ibuprofen's most common side effect is stomach irritation, which can be minimized by taking it on a full stomach and with plenty of water.

Aspirin also has a place in the first-aid kit, less as a painkiller than as an anticoagulant. Doctors have long recommended that survivors of a heart attack ingest one aspirin a day to help keep their blood pumping more easily. More recently, it was discovered that chewing an aspirin at the onset of a heart attack can lessen its severity and the damage it does to cardiac tissue.

Antihistamines

A good antihistamine belongs in every modern field first-aid kit, and the one I've liked best so far is diphenhydramine HCI, best known as Benadryl. Benadryl capsules and ointment are sold over the counter at drugstores, and if space permits, I recommend including both in your kit.

While most often used as a remedy for sinusitis caused by hay fever, Benadryl capsules reduce systemic reactions to bee stings and spider or insect bites. Used together, ointment and capsules provide good relief from the torment of poison ivy and other skin allergies. Diphenhydramine also provides an atropinelike effect that helps ward off the effects of nerve agents, which are found not only in military weapons but also in many household and agricultural pesticides. Benadryl's most common side effects are drowsiness and a dry mouth.

Antiseptics

Tincture of iodine has been a staple of first-aid kits for as long as I can recall. Doctors no longer recommend liquid iodine for disinfecting minor skin injuries, because while it does kill all known bacteria and viruses, it also destroys the topmost layer of live skin cells (that's why it stings).

Iodine's most important use in the wilderness has historically been for water purification. Three drops per quart of water (maximum) will kill *Giardia lamblia,* but some parasitic pathogens, namely *Cryptosporidium* and *Cyclospora,* can remain viable and infectious in iodine concentrations that are toxic to humans. I still pack bottled iodine on the trail, because no current water filter can strain out viruses, and iodized water is safer to drink than untreated water if my filter should fail. Mix the iodized water well by sharing the canteen, sloshing some over its mouth, and wait 15 minutes before drinking.

Too, iodine is an important trace nutrient in the human diet, with a recommended daily allowance of 150 micrograms. Iodine helps keep the thyroid gland healthy, helps regulate the body's internal temperature, and aids in the absorption of oxygen. Ingestion also provides some protection against radiation poisoning, and iodine has been a staple in the diet of Russia's Chernobyl survivors since that tragedy occured.

Antidiarrheals

Diarrhea is a common affliction among campers. Sometimes the culprit is a waterborne parasite, but most often a dysfunctional digestive tract is caused simply by a change in diet. Several days of eating freeze-dried camping foods causes some degree of bowel upset in most backpackers, and kids especially have been getting bellyaches from gorging themselves on wild fruits since time began.

Whatever its cause, diarrhea can become a real problem when miles of trail lay before you. You might not be able to cure the affliction causing diarrhea, but you can lessen the severity of its symptoms with an oral drug called loperamide HCl, better known as Imodium AD.

Loperamide hydrochloride works by slowing the progress of food through the digestive tract, effectively reducing the amount of excreta that reaches the bowels. In real terms this means you won't be dropping your pack and running for the bushes every few minutes, and that's a tremendous relief by itself.

FIRST-AID KIT HARDWARE

Standard tools for the field first-aid kit include a quality toenail clipper for trimming hangnails and calluses, a good tweezer for pulling splinters, and a small, sharp scissors for cutting away clothing and bandages. A packet of sewing needles is handy for lancing blisters, and there should be a half-dozen safety pins in different sizes for fastening bandages and elastic wraps.

VITAMIN TABLETS

Finally, I like having a supply of quality multivitamins to keep the body's immune system working at optimal efficiency. That even well-fed backpackers typically return to civilization several pounds lighter after a weeklong outing is an indication of how much energy is required for life in the wild. Since good health is always the best defense against infection, it pays to keep a hardworking body well supplied with usable nutrients.

Centrum is the brand of vitamin I usually backpack with, mainly because it has higher concentrations of nutrients than most, but any good multivitamin will suffice (one comedian claims to carry children's Flintstones vitamins when traveling to avoid problems with customs agents). The trick lies in getting these nutrients out of the pill and into your system.

Because I know a fellow with the unenviable occupation of readying portable toilets for their next engagement, I've learned that many vitamin capsules pass through the digestive system more or less intact. This problem can be remedied by chewing the vitamin as thoroughly as you can stand before swallowing it with as much water as you can hold.

THE KIT

The last step is to pack these and any other medical items you think might be necessary into a container that will keep them easily accessible, yet protected from damage and the elements.

The options here are many: My day pack carries a surprisingly complete medical kit inside a plastic videotape box; my wife prefers hers inside a zip-open case originally meant for audio cassettes; two of my larger backpacks carry fanny-pack kits that have worked well for traveling quickly on foot to the scene of a medical emergency; and the shoulder-bag kit in my 4x4 makes a much better first-aid kit than it ever did a camera bag. Small items should be further segregated and protected inside zipper-lock plastic bags to make their contents easy to identify, and to prevent possible spills, punctures, or contamination from other items.

My finger is healed now, but I know that wasn't the last time I or one of my companions will sprain, break, or try to lop off some part of our anatomies in the woods. I don't look forward to dealing with these injuries, but I'd purely dread trying to treat any of them without a well-provisioned first-aid kit.

6

Survival Tools

Many animals use tools: Otters break open mussels with rocks, chimpanzees catch ants using a blade of grass, and some shorebirds pound captured snails against stones to open their shells.

But only humans have sufficient capacity for imagination to first envision and then understand that four poles bound together at their tops and spread equidistantly at their bottoms can become the frame of a basic tepee shelter. Or that a strip of animal hide tied under stress across the length of a springy sapling forms a flexible bow capable of hurtling wooden missiles with lethal force. Every beaver knows how to dam up a running stream, but only a human can build a waterwheel to harness its energy.

An apparent sacrifice for our bigger and more complex brain is that humans lack many of the physical tools and abilities most other animals are born with. No other creature has cause to fear the elements as we do, and almost none suffers the acute night blindness that has forced our species to become creatures of daylight. Our stubby nose is virtually senseless, our ears are mostly ornamental, and we cannot duplicate the magnetic sense of direction that seems almost universal among our "lower" cousins. When it comes to survival in a wholly natural setting, we really are naked apes, and no human has ever survived for long without manufactured tools.

Few people get themselves stranded in a wilderness wearing only their underwear, and while the most effective primitive methods are covered in this book, an intelligent outdoorsman will always be prepared for problems. No animal is without resources, nor were the Indians and frontiersmen who roamed the New World when it was a vast wilderness, and it behooves us to follow their examples, especially today, when outdoor equipment is better and more effective than ever.

Perhaps just as bad as not having a piece of survival gear when you need it is lugging items that have little or no value. Following are the items that I personally rate important enough to carry alone or in a survival backpack, ranked in order of importance.

SURVIVAL KNIVES

Among mammals, only our species was not endowed with meaningful physical tools for digging, cutting, tearing, gouging, or stabbing. Birds have beaks, cats have fangs, bears have claws, and deer have hooves, because an instrument with which to perform these tasks is essential to life in a natural environment.

Our species' basic answer to having been denied teeth and claws is a knife. More than any other piece of outdoor equipment, a sharp and sturdy belt knife capable of withstanding hard duty should be on your hip anytime you aren't sleeping. I draw and resheath my knife more than a dozen times a day to cut rope, saw notches, whittle a tent stake, or snag a boiling cooking pot by its wire handle. With a stout, sharp survival knife, you can chop, whittle, pound, and process foods. Without it, performing any of these simple tasks ranges from difficult to impossible.

While any knife beats having none in a survival situation, today's pure-blooded survival knives are designed to do a lot more than just cut. Because a survival knife must not break under any strain its user can physically inflict, all have heavy, virtually indestructible blades with a full tang (the portion of the blade inside the handle) that extends through a nonslip handle for maximum prying strength. All are stamped or cast from alloys that will take and hold a keen edge, then precision heat-treated to obtain an ideal hardness

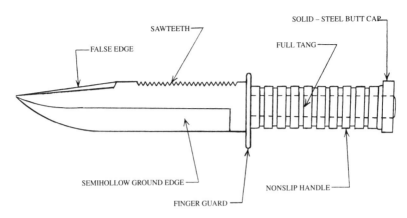

BOWIE-TYPE SURVIVAL KNIFE.

and toughness. The features that I consider most important include a solid butt cap that allows the knife to be used as a hammer, saw-teeth along the blade's spine for cutting notches, and a sheath fitted with, or capable of carrying, cargo pockets to contain other survival tools.

Today's fully outfitted survival knives live up to the name better than ever. Each of my own carries a sheath kit that includes a fire starter, pocket compass, and Maglite AAA Solitaire flashlight, all tied to the sheath with a foot of nylon string. Several feet of stout cord wrapped around the sheath bottom helps complete the outfit. I've come to rely heavily on this survival knife system in recent years. Every tool it carries has proven its value many times over, and when I'm in the woods, my knife is always the first thing I put on after my boots each morning.

FOLDING SURVIVAL KNIVES

The rather large woman hanging from her shoulder belt on the passenger side of the upside-down Ford LTD was stuck. Neither she nor the man who had crawled inside through the shattered driver's-side window could reach the belt's release catch. The dazed guy pulling mindlessly against the woman's arm from her other side wasn't helping much either.

Worse, I could smell and hear gasoline sizzling against hot exhaust pipes, and it was enough to pucker portions of my anatomy. When I'd arrived with my truck first-aid kit, everyone at the scene was searching for something sharp enough to sever the seat belt. Meanwhile the woman, who could smell and hear the sizzling of gasoline as well as I could, was getting a little frantic. I snapped open my Buck CrossLock, slashed the seat belt in two with a single stroke, and we pulled the sobbing woman through the window to safety.

Not every survival problem occurs in the wilderness. While a fixed-blade survival knife can be made to perform almost any cutting job, there will always be routine chores that are better accomplished by a smaller and less unwieldy blade. The same beefiness that gives a survival knife its strength works against it when the task at hand involves cleaning fish, whittling, slicing vegetables, or removing a splinter from your finger. Aside from the obvious impracticality of carrying a sheath knife in civilized company, there are many tasks for which the delicate touch of a razor-keen edge is more useful than brute strength and size.

Bush Knives

Bush knives are large, strong blades whose length and weight make them a nearly ideal chopping tool. Traditionally, north woodsmen have preferred the power and brute strength of a hatchet for manipulating hard woods. In the Tropics nothing beats the longer and slimmer machete for penetrating the lianas and bamboo of a tropical jungle. But a conventional machete's blade is prone to breakage when pitted against wood, while the abbreviated cutting edge of a hatchet is all but useless for hacking through undergrowth.

Knife makers had been aware of the functionality gap between machete and hatchet, but they had to wait for manufacturing technology to catch up with their ideas before they could remedy the problem. Today, better steels and faster, less expensive production processes have made possible designs that effectively combine the best features of both tools. As a result, there are many brands and shapes of bush knife on the market, all of them short enought to be swung without interference in thick country, heavy enough to deliver a powerful chopping blow, and stout enough to be called unbreakable. These are not survival knives in the same sense as a belt knife, but you'll find a well-used bush knife strapped to the side of my backpack whenever I plan to be gone overnight or longer.

COMPASSES

The first thing you need to know about buying a compass is that humans have no natural sense of direction. Some people have always insisted otherwise, but no one has yet proven this assertion. A few have suffered and even died from the trying, however, so a good compass should be considered absolutely vital for anyone venturing into the woods. With a compass, the greenest novice can always know in which direction home lies; without it, even an expert woodsman is never far from lost in a canopied forest.

Well-made but inexpensive compasses abound these days, so there is no reason to settle for second best with this vital instrument. All of my own compasses have liquid-filled indicator capsules to provide fast, smooth movement without the annoying needle bounce common to unfilled models. The indicator needle or dial must rotate smoothly, with no hint of stickiness, when the compass is laid flat and its body turned; the magnet should be strong enough to follow a paper clip or penknife blade in a complete circle. The liquid-filled capsule of a new compass should have no air bubbles of any size inside; air bubbles can occur over time from repeated exposure to temperature extremes, but a bubble inside a new compass can mean a leaky indicator capsule. You can count on the bubble to grow in size until it blocks the indicator from turning and renders the instrument useless.

Avoid the traditional pin-on "hunter's" compass. Aside from being an archaic and inherently unreliable design, pin-on compasses can almost be counted on to disappear from their moorings at the most inopportune time. The place for a working compass is around your neck, inside your shirt or jacket.

MAPS

Anytime you venture into the boondocks, you should have a map of the area you're traveling, even if you never leave a trail. A map is essentially just an aerial picture of the surrounding countryside, giving you a preview of terrain features ahead of or around your position. With a map and compass, you can determine your location by using identifiable landmarks and plot a safer course through rugged terrain, because you'll know what's there before you arrive. Hikers tend to take this advantage for granted in an era when every foot of the planet has been mapped, but not a half century has passed since large regions of the earth were just blank spots labeled UNEXPLORED TERRITORY.

While I consider an area map necessary in any location, how useful it will be depends on the terrain. Survival instructors in the western United States generally consider a map more important than a compass, because the country is open and dotted with prominent, easily identifiable landmarks. In the deep woods, where anything beyond 50 yards is out of sight and getting completely turned around can happen in areas smaller than some backyards, a compass is indispensable. A savvy survivalist always has both.

While even a filling-station road map is better than none at all, the dividends paid from having a map made for travel in the wilderness cannot be overstated. A snowmobiler will probably be most interested in the locations and destinations of designated snowmobile trails, which typically follow established hiking trails and seasonal roads, and usually aren't marked on any topographic maps. The same applies to cross-country skiing and summer backpacking.

Maps from the U.S. Geographical Survey (USGS) in Washington, D.C., are necessarily macrocosmic and can't reflect changes that may have occurred in every area since their printing. I don't suggest leaving behind your USGS topo, but it's never dumb to contact local conservation or park authorities for an updated trail map and conditions report before embarking on any wilderness excursion.

Colored, almost framable, topographic maps can be purchased by mail. Write to:

U.S. Geographical Survey
Information Services
P.O. Box 25286
Denver, CO 80225

These very detailed topos are priced at $4 each, with a shipping-and-handling fee of $3.50 per order, so it pays to buy several at once.

Internet users may also benefit from on-line map servers, although the best and most detailed maps are never available without cost. The Northern Michigan Wolf Detection and Habitat Survey Team, on which I serve as tracker, was given detailed maps from the Odawa tribe's Natural Resources Commission. Yet none clearly showed the concentric postglacial dunes, now heavily forested, that line the shoreline of Lake Michigan's Sturgeon Bay. I did find these, however, on Microsoft's Terraserver Web site (www.terraserver.com), a compilation of zoomable satellite photos that revealed unusual terrain features we hadn't been aware of, despite having transected the area several times on foot.

FIRE-STARTING KIT

The temperature was 20 degrees F and falling when my friend slipped backward off an icy log and plunged into a deep spring-fed stream. His cotton long johns and down parka were immediately saturated, and within seconds of being pulled from the water he was doubled over with hypothermia-induced stomach cramps. We were 3 miles from the truck, and just 200 yards from camp, but an all-day freezing rain had coated everything with a glaze of slick ice.

Such conditions were the stuff of nightmares for previous generations of woodsmen, but five minutes after he was half dragged into camp, my friend was warming himself next to a crackling fire.

No survival skill has more potential for saving your life anywhere on the planet than an ability to quickly make fire under any weather conditions. Prolonged exposure to temperatures below 50 degrees F without adequate clothing can kill within hours. Throw in a hard rain, and evaporative cooling increases the danger zone to as high as 70 degrees. Few places on earth are consistently warm enough for naked apes to survive long without fire. Add the fact that a warm fire, kept bright or smoky as conditions demand, is a lost or stranded woodsman's best chance for alerting help, and this ageless skill is as critical to survival today as it was in primitive times.

Several fire-starting tools made for outdoorsmen are on the market today, but only two, the Blast Match and Strike Force from Survival, Inc., have served well enough to merit a permanent place in my kit. Both models are based in principle on the time-honored flint-and-steel kits carried for centuries by frontiersmen and Indians, except much improved by modern manufacturing and materials.

SURVIVAL BIVYS

Bivy shelters are a modern ultralight solution to being caught in foul weather far from civilization. Sometimes known as minimalist shelters, most are barely larger than their intended occupant. As a base camp shelter, the small interior dimensions of a bivy can make it seem claustrophobic after a few days, but a typical packed weight of less than 3 pounds makes it the most functional folding domicile yet conceived.

The attributes of a good bivy shelter are essentially applicable to all tents. Taped factory-sealed seams are a must for keeping out pounding rains. Windows and doors should be large enough to provide ventilation and have bugproof inner liners of no-see-um mesh. Zippers around doors and windows must be heavy, rugged, and smooth, because a broken zipper can have serious consequences in a howling snowstorm or when mosquitoes fill the air in whining clouds. Poles should be aluminum, if available, and treated with care at all times regardless of their construction. If possible, the shelter should be freestanding, meaning that it doesn't require stakes to remain erect, but there are few places even on rock or deep snow where tension points can't be staked or tied off. Floors should be bathtub type, with extra waterproofing that extends upward about 4 inches from the ground to protect occupants and gear from rainwater runoff. All of this might sound like a lot to ask from an ultralight emergency shelter, but several survival bivys meet all these criteria, with prices ranging from about $100 to more than twice that amount.

BEDROLLS

For more than a decade, my four-season bedroll consisted of a six-point heavyweight woolen trade blanket. In summer I folded and doubled the big 7-pound blanket to form a sleeping pad, covering up with the topmost layer if the night got cold. In winter I'd make a bed from body-length dead logs and branches laid side by side atop the snow, then sleep on top rolled inside my blanket like a cocooned caterpillar.

I didn't particularly like carrying this heavy blanket, but it rolled up compactly enough and I could trust it to keep me warm in every season. Being wool, it had natural water-repellent qualities, but even exposed to a pouring rain it still retained at least half its warmth. It dried quickly, and I could tie it erect between the trees behind me to serve as a heat reflector and windbreak while it dried. Mostly, though, I carried this time-honored bedroll of the voyageurs and Indians because I had already suffered when my down-filled bag took a dunking that reduced it to a sack of sodden, lumped-together feathers.

Today I use and recommend modern synthetic-fill sleeping bags in any season, and especially for the survival backpack. Despite many proprietary names and arrangements, one common factor among better synthetic sleeping-bag fills is insulation comprised of hollow plastic fibers that are inherently waterproof. These tiny hollow tubes are divided into chambers inside, then layered and bonded to one another in different configurations to create numerous efficiency levels, trademark labels, and price ranges.

All of these synthetic fills are water repellent and retain about 75 percent of their efficiency when wet, and a 15-degree bag stuffed with Hollofil is every bit as warm as a 15-degree bag filled with higher-priced Polarguard HV. The differences are weight and cost: The lighter and more compactible a sleeping bag is in a given temperature range, the heavier will be its impact on your wallet. It might seem to defy logic to pay more for less, but in general the heavier the sleeping bag, the lower its price tag.

Hallmarks of a sleeping bag made for serious use include a heavy YKK-brand zipper that can be vented through the foot if needed, with a thick draft tube running its entire length on the inside. In better bags the zipper is edged inside with a ribbon of stiff fabric that holds the liner away from the zipper teeth to keep it from snagging the lining while you open or close the bag.

Like backpackers, most folks outfitting for survival will find a sleeping bag in the 15-degree range to be their happiest medium in a four-season climate. If you wear pac-boot liners, long underwear, a sweater, and a knit hat to bed, you can use a 15-degree bag at 0 degrees F without losing sleep.

In subzero weather I sometimes supplement the roughly 4-pound weight of a 15-degree mummy bag with a 1.5-pound fleece liner of polypropylene fabric. These retail for as little as $6 each at sporting goods outlets, but better models made from 200-weight fleece and heavyweight zippers average about $18. A good polypro liner lowers the comfort rating of any sleeping bag at least 15 degrees.

WATER FILTERS

Portable water-filtration devices have proven their worth in my wilderness kit over the past decade, and every survival outfit I own carries one. All must meet EPA requirements that mandate minimum removal of 99.9999 percent of bacteria and 99.9 percent of protozoan and flagellate parasites, and all will greatly reduce or remove chemical contaminants. The design of all is such that a filter produces potable water from its outlet; if it fails to, it's plugged and needs cleaning (per manufacturer's instructions).

While it's true that these figures don't guarantee removal of every single organism, they were based on the fact that such low concentrations are easily handled by an average immune system. None can remove viruses, which are too small to be filtered out, but these are almost never found in nature, and they can be easily killed in suspect water either by boiling or by the addition of three drops of liquid iodine (maximum) per quart of water. Today, after nearly two decades of service with no illnesses reported, it seems like an unnecessary hardship not to have the ability to draw drinking water from any mud puddle, alkaline water hole, or scum-covered pond. Available models range from water-bottle types with a built-in filter that removes bugs from raw water inside with just a squeeze of the bottle to a variety of pump types that can produce potable water in large quantities.

SURVIVAL FLASHLIGHTS

The sun had set when I hit the halfway point of my 7-mile trek to rendezvous with Odawa tribal biologists the following morning, and with it air temperatures had plummeted toward a nighttime low of –12 degrees F. The cedar swamp that lay between me and my intended camp was dark, despite having 3 feet of hardpack snow on the ground, and the trail I was snowshoeing had not been broken in a month of heavy snows. In many places all that kept me on the trail was pale blue diamonds painted onto tree trunks, and those were getting tough to see in the swiftly waning light.

I reached for the holster on my hip, which always carries an AA Mini-Mag flashlight, and immediately uttered a string of expletives when I discovered that it was empty. I knew where my flashlight was: tied with a slipknot to an overhead ring in my tent, where it had served as a reading lamp the previous night. Unfortunately, my tent was in the bottom of my backpack, and I had no intention of unpacking it before I got to camp.

Backup time: I unwound the AAA Solitaire flashlight in my knife sheath from its attached lanyard. It served as a reliable trail guide for the next two hours in subzero temperatures.

A lot of people get "lost" in the woods for no other reason than underestimating how much time it will take to complete their intended circuit. Overstaying their anticipated time on the trail is common among novices and professionals alike, and without a source of light to guide them through a darkened wood, both are well advised to stay put until morning. It doesn't matter whether or not you were lost when the sun set; what matters is that you will almost certainly end up that way if you try to navigate a night forest without artificial light. And you might get a twisted ankle or branch in your eyeball in the process. Contrary to western novels, it was never superstition that kept Indians from hunting or fighting at night, but rather firsthand knowledge of the dangers inherent to attempting such things when effectively blind.

7

Miscellaneous Survival
Techniques

A true-life survival scenario that can affect virtually anyone is loss of utilities and the luxuries that all of us have learned to take for granted. Not long ago a power outage forced the manager of a local supermarket to close its doors for several hours. Having the store's electronic cash registers, office computers, and bar-code scanners out of commission made conducting modern-day business impossible. He sent all but a skeleton crew home and waited for the lights to come back on.

After about 15 minutes under the dim glow of emergency floodlights the manager, a bright and well-educated man, announced that he was going to make some popcorn for them all to snack on while they waited. He snatched a bag of microwave popcorn from the shelf and marched straight to the lunchroom at the back of the store. He returned a minute later, red faced and sheepish.

As this story illustrates, modern humans are conditioned—maybe even enslaved—to conveniences of our own making. But our hold on technology in daily life is tenuous, and when conveniences are denied, as they often can be due to a power outage or act of nature, it pays to have a few extra survival tricks up your sleeve.

SURVIVAL KNOTS

Rope has always been a necessary part of the human survival kit because it provides the means to fasten objects together and fashion simple machines. This means you must also have a working knowledge of basic knots to ensure that you choose the proper one for the application. An improperly tied knot can be dangerous, coming apart under stress or tightening into a compressed mass that may be impossible to untie.

Square Knot

This is the workhorse knot used by every person who knows how to tie a pair of shoes. It's the best knot for fastening the ends of two ropes together; it won't slip under a heavy pull, yet a square

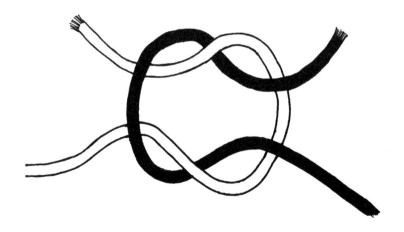

SQUARE KNOT

knot remains relatively easy to untie even after being pulled against. The only hazard to be avoided is improperly crossing either end, which results in "granny knot" that's both untrustworthy under a load and sometimes virtually impossible to get untied.

Double Half Hitch

This is the classic slipknot, used for fastening the end of a rope to itself to form a noose that slides closed when pulled against, becoming tighter and harder to loosen as more force is applied. A double half hitch is the best choice for snares and traps, but it works well for fastening shelter frames together.

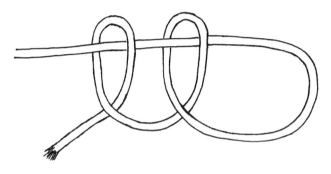

DOUBLE HALF-HITCH SLIPKNOT

Bowline

This is the knot used to form those nontightening loops that sailors throw over pilings to secure the bow of a boat when docking, hence its name. A bowline can also be used to secure ropes

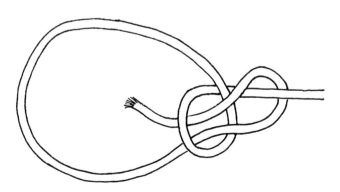

BOWLINE KNOT

around rescue victims who must be hauled to safety, and it's the simplest way to tie a nonslip loop around a tree or any object that you can't get over or under with an already-tied loop.

Timber Hitch

Back in the days when lumberjacking meant knowing how to drive a team of workhorses to "skid" logs out of a forest, every timber cutter knew how to fasten a timber hitch. A chain, cable, or hauser tied to a limbless tree trunk using a simple slipknot will slide over and free of the trunk as it's being dragged, so log skidders added a second simple loop ahead of the slipknot. This "locking loop" is secured to the tree by the slipknot loop, which, although not secure enough to hold by itself, provides enough of an anchor to make the simple loop tighten like a garrote. Applications for this very handy knot are limited only by conditions and necessity, but one of its best uses, I think, is suspending an ultralight mesh hammock from between two smooth-trunked trees when camping.

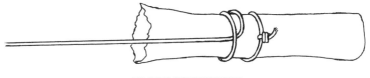

TIMBER HITCH KNOT

Cattail Rope

I've always recommended that survivalists include several yards of 550-pound-test parachute cord in their kits, because no natural materials can match it for strength, abrasion resistance, and all-around performance. But because parachute cord can have such tremendous value in a genuine survival dilemma, there are good reasons to conserve it as much as possible. Fortunately, cattails, which are found growing along the shorelines of nearly every body of fresh water in the world, make a very good field-expedient rope that works adequately for most tasks that require rope. A four-strand (about ½-inch) rope made from cattail fibers can suspend up to 100 pounds, ties well, and will actually remain usable for several years unless left to rot in the elements.

Beginning with a single cattail leaf about 4 feet long, split the leaf lengthwise down its middle. Place both halves between your palms and roll them back and forth forcefully to separate the leaf's tough fibers. Continue the rolling process until the entire length has been crushed and its fibers exposed.

1. SPLITTING THE LEAF

2. FASTENING LEAF HALVES TOGETHER

3. FIRST TWIST-LOCK

TWISTING THE TIED ENDS

Next, tie the narrow ends of the two halves together several inches from their ends using a square knot or double half hitch. It isn't important that this knot be tight, because all it must do is hold the halves together as they're twist-locked and doubled.

Stand on one end of the tied-together leaf to hold it firmly in place and begin twisting its upper end in a clockwise direction. (It doesn't actually matter in which direction you twist, so long as each section is twisted in the same direction at each stage of the rope-making process.) As you twist, the leaf will become shorter and more uniform along its length. Smooth out bumps by rolling them between your forefinger and thumb. Continue twisting until the

4. DOUBLING THE TWISTED-LEAF

5. SPLICING TWO TWIST-LOCKED LENGTHS TOGETHER

6. COMPLETE ROPE MAY BE FURTHER DOUBLED AND TWIST-LOCKED

MAKING CATTAIL ROPE

leaves, which are already beginning to look like cord, exhibit a tendency to coil around themselves when tension on them is eased. If the leaf breaks apart (nearly always in its center), just tie the ends together again and start over.

Bend the twisted strand in its middle by grasping the center and upper end firmly between your thumb and forefinger, then bringing the upper end down evenly with the lower. Hold both the ends firmly together and carefully allow the now-doubled center to twist in a counterclockwise direction (presuming the original twist was clockwise). You'll see that the doubled strand twist-locks around itself and stays that way so long as the ends are held. Left alone, the loose ends will unravel two or three turns, but that's okay: You'll need loose ends for splicing later. Make several of these twist-locked doubled lengths, each of which will probably average 3 to 4 feet long.

Take two of these lengths and splice them together by taking the loose ends of one and threading them through the loop formed at the twisted end of the other. Unwind the turn directly below that end loop and insert the loose ends through the hole that this makes, again from opposite directions. Continue the process until the ends have been crisscrossed at least three times through the coils of the other length. Friction will hold the spliced ends in place, gripping them tighter as more force is exerted against the rope.

After splicing together several lengths, the final step in making them into rope is to once again twist-lock and halve the assembled length. Since this is likely to be 8 to 10 feet—too long to step on and twist—I drive a wooden stake (dead tree branch) into the earth and fit the looped end over its top to hold it in place as I twist the opposite end. Another wooden stake in the center of the cord works as the fulcrum for bending the twisted length in half.

At this point you'll know in which direction to twist, because twisting in the wrong direction will unwind the coils. Instead, tighten them with several more turns, then bend the length around the center stake, bringing your end around to the opposite end. Maintain tension against both ends as you ease the looped end off its stake. With both ends free, carefully allow them to twist-lock evenly around themselves down to and around the remaining stake. Splice together the ends in your hands and you have roughly 4 feet of ½-inch rope for lashing together a shelter or any other medium-duty jobs for which you wouldn't want to cut a piece of parachute cord. Several finished lengths can be spliced together to make a longer rope, or they can be twist-locked and spliced again to make a stronger rope.

KNIFE AND TOOL SHARPENING

"A dull knife'll cut you quicker than a sharp one." This bit of deer-skinner wisdom is more true than it might seem. The problem is that human skin is fragile in comparison to the wood, rubber hose, or wet rope a working knife might be pitted against, and the duller a blade is, the harder you'll need to push downward to sever tough materials. The harder you push, the more likely you are to slip. The sharper the knife, the less effort will be needed to cut the same material.

Anatomy of a Cutting Edge

The blades of all single-edge knives are comprised of three essential parts. The spine, or top, unsharpened portion of the blade is full thickness to provide strength. Below the spine is a ground edge, applied at the factory, that largely determines how strong or sharp the blade can be made (generally speaking, an increase in one of

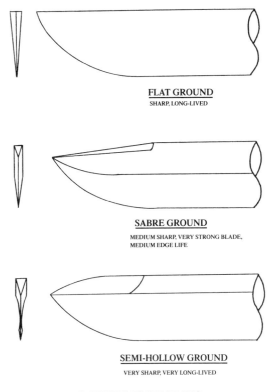

FLAT GROUND
SHARP, LONG-LIVED

SABRE GROUND
MEDIUM SHARP, VERY STRONG BLADE,
MEDIUM EDGE LIFE

SEMI-HOLLOW GROUND
VERY SHARP, VERY LONG-LIVED

SURVIVAL KNIFE EDGES

these characteristics decreases the other). Last is the honed edge, or cutting edge, the part that you'll be directly concerned with during the sharpening process.

Seen in cross section, the ground edge of a single-edge knife appears as a tall, narrow V, more or less. The taller (and therefore the narrower) the V is at its point, the sharper will be the honed edge, and the longer it will stay sharp.

Honing Stones

Aluminum oxide is the honing stone most people know best, a gritty gray-colored block, sometimes a disk, of abrasive man-made material. This is the cutting stone of a honing kit, used to grind flat a cutting edge on each side to form a rough but even V that can then be smoothed with harder, less coarse oilstones. A functional edge can be obtained from an aluminum oxide stone alone, but shaving sharpness requires additional polishing.

Unlike oilstones—which actually work better when lubricated with water—an aluminum oxide stone must never be oiled, or it will be ruined forever. Not being true stone, aluminum oxide absorbs and permanently holds oils. Honing against such a surface forms a hard, slippery glaze of steel, stone, and oil that will neither sharpen a blade, wash out, nor become anything except a worse problem. Use only water as a cutting medium for any aluminum oxide honing stone.

True oilstones are cut from natural rock, the best known of these coming from Arkansas, and are usually available in medium (gray) and fine (white) coarsenesses. Neither is abrasive enough to sharpen a blade that doesn't already have a nice V-shaped cutting edge, but either can polish an existing edge to shaving sharpness.

Power grinders and belt sanders are to be avoided, especially where knives are concerned. Both remove far too much metal, and even professional machinists cannot control the angle of a blade being ground. Many fine knives have been aesthetically destroyed with a single pass against a bench grinder.

Honing Methods

The first step in sharpening any cutting edge, whether on a lawn-mower blade, ax, or knife, is applying the primary edge—a flat, even surface on each side of the blade that forms a sharp V shape when viewed end-on. Various methods have been described for accomplishing this task, but the bottom line is that whatever angle or stroke is used, an evenly honed primary edge will be sharp enough to handle most cutting jobs with no further work.

Having said that, the most accepted honing stroke is to rotate the primary edge against an aluminum oxide stone as if you're trying to slice a thin layer from the stone's surface. Again, the angle isn't really important—I normally change mine to a steeper and sharper V than the factory edge anyway—but it's critical that both sides be flat and even. For the sake of convenience, I recommend

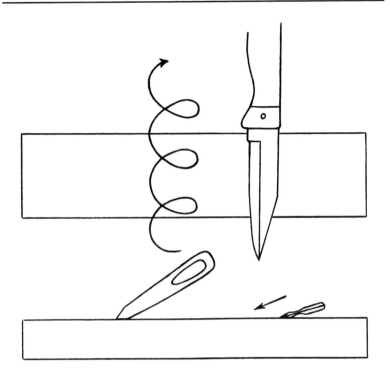

SHARPENING TOOLS AGAINST A STONE

following the same angle used by the factory until you've mastered resharpening a dull blade.

Beginners typically complain that their knife isn't getting sharper, or even that it seems to be getting duller as they hone. Once again, the problem always lies with the V of the primary edge. When stroked flat against a stone, the primary edge will exhibit a steady, even drag under gentle pressure, with none of the slippery spots or "chattering" that result from holding the blade at an angle different from the edge. Keeping the stone wet with clear water will increase its abrasiveness and help you feel when the cutting edge is flat against its surface. If the edge doesn't feel sharp, either your angle is wrong or you haven't worked the steel enough to form a proper V.

EMERGENCY SNOWSHOES

In 1991 more than 100 survival students were rescued from the normally snow-free Smoky Mountains after a freak blizzard took the state of Tennessee by complete surprise. I spoke at length with a young fellow who'd been a student in that survival course, and the stories he related of panicked instructors abandoning their students in the storm were enough to give me goose bumps. Fortunately, normal winter temperatures of about 50 degrees F returned quickly, but the National Guard spent three days plucking the scattered students from where deep snow had kept them stranded.

Making field-expedient snowshoes is a skill that every survivalist in snow country should know. As these students learned the hard way, drifted waist-deep snow is effectively impassable without some type of foot extension that spreads its wearer's weight over a greater surface area. Distributing your weight over more area means the number of pounds per square inch being exerted against a surface will decrease, the effect being to make you weigh less so far as snow underfoot is concerned.

The snowshoes shown here are simple to construct from almost any environment where they might be needed. With no decking, they will sink a bit deeper than manufactured snowshoes that have a deck (more surface area), but they will provide enough flotation on even powder snow to ensure that you're never stranded.

I believe the illustrations given here are self-explanatory so far as design is concerned, but there are a few helpful tips that don't show in a drawing. First, all frame members should be made from green wood, namely tree saplings, because it's important that a snowshoe frame be springy to keep it from breaking underfoot—one snowshoe is no snowshoes at all. All frame pieces should be at least 1 inch in diameter, and all joints should be slightly notched to help lock them tightly into place with as few wraps of cord as possible. The overall length of the snowshoe should depend on snow consistency and depth—longer for increased flotation on deep snow, shorter on hardpack—but I recommend a minimum finished length of no less than 4 feet. Each finished 'shoe should be tail-heavy, its rear dragging slightly as the foot is brought forward, to help keep it tracking straight through the snow.

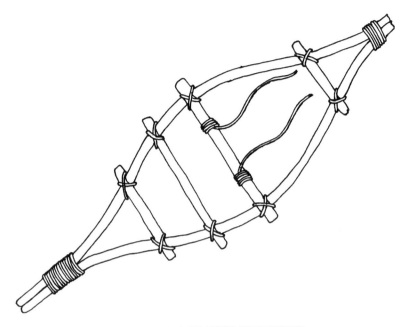

OJIBWA-TYPE EMERGENCY SNOWSHOE

As shown, bindings are a simple wraparound affair made from rope. In fact, these rope bindings are probably the equal of most conventional leather types, but I recommend tying them with a looped square knot like that used to tie shoelaces. The binding isn't likely to come untied, but it's a good bet that the rope will absorb water and freeze the knot solid, so it pays to have a knot that comes apart with a yank.

Using field-expedient snowshoes is little different from wearing most traditional wood-and-leather models. No real skill is required, but your feet should be centered on the arch members and the bindings tied snugly. As with all snowshoes, walking requires first raising the 'shoe's nose above the snow surface before bringing that foot straight forward. Flotation can be increased by tying a web of rope, or even strips of cloth, across the frame members, leaving enough clearance at the toes to allow the snowshoe to swivel freely downward at the tail when that foot is raised.

BEATING THE BUGS

Northern lumberjacks of old sometimes suffered from an affliction they knew as swamp madness, which according to some accounts caused those afflicted to go utterly insane and run screaming through the forest.

In fact, swamp madness was a simple nervous breakdown brought on by 12-hour days of brutally hard labor, hordes of biting bugs 24-hours a day, and sleep deprivation, culminating in a state of total physical and mental exhaustion. The sickness passed completely once a victim was returned to town, where civilization had destroyed the habitats and breeding grounds of most mosquitoes, horseflies, deerflies, stable flies, and blackflies.

Like all true bugs, these annoying insects are distinguished by a hollow proboscis designed for penetrating and sucking nourishment from a living host. Some bugs, like the weevils, attack only plants, while others require animal blood to procreate. Some are insects, a few are arachnids, many can fly, but some must crawl. Most are known to attack in great starving hordes, and every species is at best a great torment to its victims.

Mosquitoes, which are actually long-horned flies of the family Culicidae, represent the best-known and most widespread of bloodsucking fliers. The three most important North American genera, *Aedes, Culex*, and *Anopheles,* are also found around the globe, from China to Africa and South America. Each is a known vector for disease, meaning that mosquitoes can pick up, carry, and subsequently inoculate their victims with diseases that range from mild to life threatening.

Most mosquitoes are active at night, but some bite by day. In deep, moist forests where both are present, the torment can be unceasing. Opportunistic feeders, the insects lie in wait on trees and vegetation until stimulated to feed by the heat, respiration, and perhaps even color of a passing victim. Blues are thought to attract mosquitoes, while subdued colors, grays especially, seem to provoke the least interest.

Only the females of any species of bug drinks blood, which provides the animal proteins necessary for development of their eggs, but males and females alike feed on pollen. Female mosquitoes feed on blood only once before flying off to lay their eggs and

BLACKFLY (FAMILY SIIMULIIDAE)

then die, but when they fill the air like snowflakes in a blizzard, you'd swear that some were coming back for seconds.

In some seasons and locations blackflies, or buffalo gnats, can be worse than mosquitoes. More than 600 species are found in temperate to tropical climes around the world, always close to a pond or lake, because blackfly females also require standing water on which to lay their eggs. Again, only females drink blood, but when they rise in great black clouds from shorelines during the spring hatch, that's plenty. By midsummer most blackflies will have mated, laid eggs, and died off, but from April to June they are the most persistent bugs on earth, crawling into ears, eyes, and nostrils and generally driving their victims to distraction.

Blackflies also are vectors for diseases dangerous to humans. Tularemia transmission has been linked to blackfly bites, and early records credit the tiny bugs with killing thousands of domestic animals in a single season. The actual bite is painless but usually

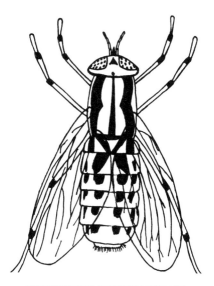

DEERFLY (FAMILY TABANIDAE)

marked by a trickle of blood. Within minutes, a dime-size wheal appears, followed by up to several days of itching. An accumulation of blackfly bites, or more specifically of the anticoagulant venom they inject while biting, can result in a systemic reaction known as anaphylactic shock, for which hospitalization is normally required.

Getting away from shaded woods and standing water is a good way to avoid most mosquitoes and blackflies, but open, sunny woods are home to the tabanids, known more commonly as horseflies and deerflies. Easily identified by large, brilliantly colored eyes, this family of strong, fast fliers is comprised of more than 2,000 species worldwide, with 300 of these occurring in North America. All are pernicious and painful biters with proboscises designed to penetrate the toughest moosehide. They can bite through clothing to leave a freely bleeding, then itching and stinging, incision that may be a ¼ inch long.

Another common bloodsucking fly is the stable fly, also known as the dog fly, and sometimes referred to as a biting housefly by victims who fall for this bug's clever disguise. Although more trimly built and a bit quicker on the wing, like the irritating but nonbiting housefly it mimics, a stable fly possesses the same razor-like proboscis as a deerfly, and its bite is no less painful.

As the name suggests, stable flies are common around live-stock pens and cattle pastures, but almost any damp and rotting plant matter is an acceptable medium for females to deposit their eggs. Decaying vegetation along shorelines can spawn hundreds of thousands of these pests, and in peak years their presence has closed entire shorelines to humans.

The stable fly has never been linked to disease transmission in humans, but because of its bloodsucking traits the smart money is on never overlooking its potential as a vector. Of more immediate importance is the stable fly's habits, which like the housefly's bring it into contact both with humans and with germ-infested rot. The painful, itchy bite of this fly might not be dangerous, but there's no telling where its feet have been.

Ticks are a group of wingless parasitic arachnids that are best known as vectors for Lyme disease, for which there is now a vaccine. But these tiny eight-legged bugs, none more than a ¼ inch long, have always had significant medical importance to humans. All ticks are capable of inoculating their victims with a broad variety of diseases, from viral and bacterial infections like spotted fever and mennigitis to bloodborne pathogens such as malaria, and even some species of parasitic worms.

Lying in wait on a blade of grass or hidden among pine needles, the tick attaches itself to a passing warm-blooded host, then burrows down to bare skin and painlessly inserts its mouthparts. After becoming engorged with blood to perhaps three times its normal diameter, a two- to three-day process, the tick drops off and lays anywhere from a few hundred to a few thousand eggs, depending on the species.

While it would have been irresponsible not to mention the potential of bloodsucking bugs to transmit disease, neither is it true to say that any of these afflictions is common. The truth is that your chances of contracting a bugborne pathogen in North America are very slim. When Lyme disease began making headlines in the mid-1980s I was a little concerned about the many ticks I'd plucked from my own hide, flicking their little embedded heads from under my skin with a pocketknife blade. But apparently not every tick bite carries disease.

Of more immediate concern is the torment bugs inflict on their victims, and the real possibility that an unprotected human might be bitten enough times to suffer a systemic reaction to the anticoagulant venom injected by all bugs when they bite. This means keeping the little monsters from getting to you in the first place.

In heavily bug-infested areas it pays to take a tip from the moose and seek higher, more exposed elevations where constant breezes keep flying insects from getting comfortable in one place.

Repellent lotions containing N-diethyl-m-toluamide (made pronounceable as the acronym DEET) held in suspension by an oily base are most popular among outdoors folks. These are moderately effective in a backyard or campground, but when the bugs are so thick you have to spit, sneeze, and rub them out of your eyes, even the highest concentration of DEET won't stop them.

Pyrethrin-based sprays made from the flower heads of the chrysanthemum (daisy family) are a field-proven favorite for treating clothing against bugs, and many people like the fact that they're derived from a natural plant source. Pyrethrin is not approved for use on bare skin, but when applied to clothing it provides up to two weeks of protection against all insects, and will even withstand several washings before losing effectiveness.

Its natural origins notwithstanding, pyrethrin is a potentially hazardous chemical that kills all bugs on contact (it's the active ingredient in pet flea sprays). Always treat clothing in an open, well-ventilated place, and avoid inhaling fumes or overspraying. Allow treated garments to dry thoroughly before handling or wearing them, and of course never use any fabric treated with pyrethrin to wipe your eyes or mouth.

Safest of all are repellent chemicals exuded through your own skin in the form of perspiration. All humans have a natural insect repellent within our bodies. This explains why Aborigines have always lived on lands where biting flies and mosquitoes are considered intolerable by visitors from places too civilized for most bugs to live. The downside is that you must be bitten enough times to activate your body's dormant defense mechanism, which isn't a bright prospect for most folks.

Garlic capsules are popular as an orally taken insect repellent, as are vitamin B_{12} capsules. Studies have shown both to be effective,

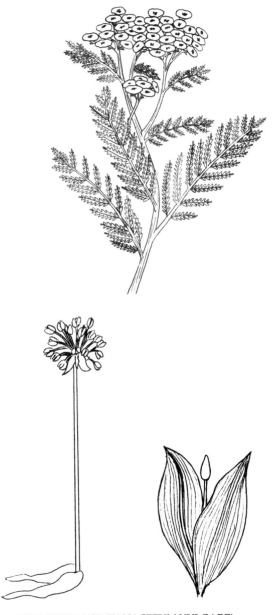

COMMON TANSY (TANACETUM VULGARE)

but personal experiences indicate that the degree of protection afforded by either depends on the number of bugs encountered.

The most valuable tool in my own bugproofing kit is a simple tube of no-see-um netting, 2 feet long by 1 foot in diameter, with an elastic band or drawstring at one end for securing it around the crown of a ball cap or bush hat. The resulting veil is inpenetrable to all bugs, yet you can see through it well enough to hike at night by flashlight; I occasionally use mine on sunny winter days as protection against snow blindness. Just keeping bugs out of your facial orifices makes them far more tolerable, and if you're hunting for supper there are no telltale chemical odors to reveal your presence. Tube veils retail for about $6 at army-navy stores, or you can make your own simply enough by sewing them from no-see-um netting, also sold at surplus stores.

Proper clothing also makes a big difference in bug country. The first rule of thumb is to wear loose clothing that moves constantly with your body movements and makes as little contact with your skin as possible. Long sleeves, rolled up or down as needed, provide a good first line of defense. Trousers should always be full length, because bare legs are a real source of torment. I prefer my ankles bloused (tied shut) to preclude invasion from that avenue.

Nor should a summer survivalist overlook wild plants that have repellent properties. As mentioned earlier, crushed flower heads of the oxeye daisy contain pyrethrin, but catnip and other mints contain oils toxic to insects in their leaves, and spicy-smelling juices from the common tansy plant are repugnant to all insects. Leeks and other wild onions are extremely repellent to bloodsucking bugs (and people), which probably explains why garlic was once commonly hung near the doors of Old World homes to repulse "vampires."

Smudge fires are small fires whose purpose it is to flood an area with dense smoke that drives away biting insects. In most cases an armful of green bracken ferns, saw grass, or pine boughs thrown onto a campfire will suffice, but in particularly bad areas I've sometimes used several smudge fires set in pits around a camp's perimeter.

Regardless of how many defenses you employ, it's a foregone conclusion that everyone who visits a summer wilderness will suffer a few bug bites. Results can range from a pox of itchy wheals that continue to torment their victims long after the fact to fever and chills in folks who are especially sensitive to the blood-thinning enzymes injected when a bug bites.

There are no cures for bug bites, only remedies. The damage has already been done and must heal naturally, ideally without further tissue destruction caused by scratching the inflamed area. The problem is that bug bites itch, so I recommend that an effective anti-itch lotion (or capsule) such as Benadryl be a seasonal part of every backwoods survival kit.

FIRE AIDS

Fire Wicks

For many years I carried the time-honored candle in my survival kit for starting fires in cold, rainy conditions that demand a source of warmth while at the same time hampering the creation of fire. A candle is of course waterproof, so it can be lit under wet conditions, and it provides a small but steady, long-burning flame to dry then ignite damp tinder.

The problem is that a whole candle is too much; all I really needed was its paraffin-saturated wick. The solution turned out to be nothing more complicated than saturating heavyweight cotton string in molten paraffin, or canning wax, then cutting it into sections after the string had cooled and stiffened. The resulting "fire wicks" are waterproof, durable enough for the survival kit, light enough to pack 100 in a pocket, and cheap enough to make certain that every vehicle and field kit containeds this many.

Two-pound blocks of paraffin can be found in most supermarkets for about $3, and you can usually find rolls of heavyweight cotton string for around $2 just a few aisles over. Do not use nylon or other synthetic strings, because they not only don't burn as hotly or as cleanly as cotton, but they emit noxious fumes as well.

A very good alternative to cotton string is woolen felt weatherstripping (or old pac-boot liners) cut into strips, then cooled and sectioned with a sharp knife. Like cotton string, the wool absorbs several times its own weight in flammable paraffin, for which it acts as a clean-burning wick. But a 1-inch block of wax-soaked felt, frayed at bit at the corner to make it easier to light, can burn steadily for five minutes, whereas cotton string fire wicks burn about one minute for a 1-inch length.

I cannot overstress the need for caution and forethought when working with molten paraffin. Hardened wax droplets are a pain to remove, so select a nonflammable work area that can withstand smoke and spills. An old saucepan placed over a hotplate in the garage is usually ideal.

Aside from accidental spills and drips, the only real danger in the process comes from overheating the paraffin. If your melting pot begins to smoke, remove it from the heat immediately, because its next step will be to burst into flame. If that does happen, cut the heat to the burner and then cover the pot with a metal lid to smother the fire.

Finished fire wicks can be stored and carried in any number of ways: cut and packed neatly in a 35-millimeter film canister, for instance, or just rolled into a sandwich bag to keep them all together. I don't know who originally thought of these nearly ideal fire starters, but they've been a permanent part of my survival kit for more than a decade.

The Buddy Burner

Liquid-fuel cookstoves were around when I was a youngster, but they sure weren't portable enough for backpacking, so I cooked my meals in the backcountry over a wood fire. But there were also times when I needed to remain undetected as well as needing a hot meal, and the scent of even a small campfire is obvious to virtually every animal within ½ mile downwind.

Then my little brother, who was seven and a Webelo Scout in 1970, showed me a nifty little cookstove he'd constructed as a troop project. It consisted of a cleaned 1-pint paint can with a kerosene lantern wick in its center, surrounded by paraffin—a giant candle in a resealable can. He told me it was called a Buddy Burner.

I lost no time copying his example, and I've been using one of these neat, inexpensive backpacking stoves as needed ever since. The first step is to precut a length of lantern wick, available at many hardware stores, long enough to extend about 1 inch above the can's rim with its lower end resting against the can's bottom. Insert two pieces of coat-hanger wire side by side through the wick at the height where they will span the can's opening on each side while keeping the wick's lower end as close to the can's bottom as possible.

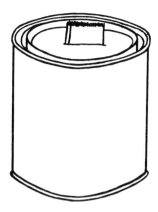

BUDDY BURNER IN A PINT-SIZED PAINT CAN

With the impaled lantern wick suspended securely across the can's center, the next and last step is to fill the paint can with molten paraffin, or canning wax. After allowing the wax to cool for three or four hours, clean any hardened paraffin you might have spilled from the paint can's lid groove and snap the top in place. The buddy burner is complete and ready for use.

A buddy burner isn't as hot as a propane or gas stove, but the pint-size model will boil a pint of water in under 10 minutes, without scent or noticeable flame, and with less bulk than a conventional backpack stove. The trick is to keep its flame out of the cooling breeze and confined in a place where nearly all of the heat it generates is directed at the cooking vessel's bottom.

I most often accomplish this by excavating a narrow slit trench deep enough for the buddy burner to sit at its bottom and still be 3 inches below ground. A cooking pot or canteen cup placed across the trench will sit securely while being heated from below, while the earthen walls of the trench help isolate the flame's heat and protect it from wind.

Extinguishing a buddy burner after use is as simple as laying its lid loosely over the can opening. I recommend waiting at least a half hour before repacking the little stove to give the paraffin inside time to reharden. Never seal the burner's lid tightly during the cooling period, because expanding gases inside will likely blow it high into the air.

Buddy burners have also proven useful for heating and lighting survival shelters. Larger versions made from quart-size paint cans have many times burned under my house, where they've always kept the water pipes from freezing in subzero weather. One fellow I used to know liked to leave a small lit buddy burner under his car's oil pan on especially cold nights as insurance that its engine would start in the morning. Once, during a winter power outage, I even used my buddy burner to heat a single closed-off room to a comfortable temperature. I can't actually recommend any of these uses in today's litigation-happy society, but they do show that a buddy burner can be a versatile tool to have in backpack, car, and home.

EMERGENCY SIGNALS

These emergency ground-to-air signals are recognized internationally. A pilot who sees them laid out on the ground with logs, scraped into a beach, or stamped into snow will know their meanings.

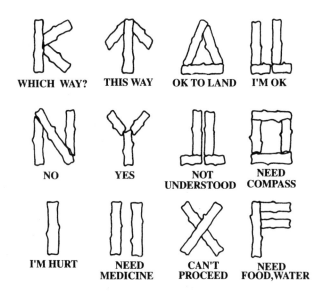

WHICH WAY?	THIS WAY	OK TO LAND	I'M OK
NO	YES	NOT UNDERSTOOD	NEED COMPASS
I'M HURT	NEED MEDICINE	CAN'T PROCEED	NEED FOOD, WATER

8

Survival Kits

Virtually everyone carries a survival kit with them at all times. Like any good survival kit, these wallets, purses, grips, and briefcases are individually equipped to cope with the most likely demands of their owners' daily lives. Almost everyone carries a driver's license or other identification and keeps small necessities like money, credit cards, and car keys on their persons during every waking hour of every normal day. In the business world a wristwatch may be vital to survival, and few people who need them leave home without eyeglasses or an asthma inhaler.

All of the above are survival items in the sense that they're necessary tools for conducting daily life in their intended environments—basically, civilization. The survival kits in this chapter address the more basic needs of human survival when the amenities and warmth of civilization are out of reach. Each is a bit specialized to better accommodate its intended use, but all meet the most basic needs of an outdoorsman in trouble. As many items as possible are expected to perform multiple tasks, and this should be a rule of thumb for everything considered for inclusion in any survival kit.

SURVIVAL KNIVES

This is my most basic and necessary survival kit. I've always considered a sharp, stout fixed-blade sheath knife to be my most essential piece of survival gear in any environment. Then Schrade spoiled me by incorporating gear pouches into the sheath of its now-defunct M7S survival knife, thereby transforming it into a truly functional stand-alone survival kit, and I've demanded them ever since. Jim Bowie's Iron Maiden might be the stuff of legends, but it didn't have nearly the utility of today's better survival knives.

Some knives, like the Schrade Extreme, have pouches incorporated into the sheath, while the same company's equally well-made Double Eagle survival knife has no provision for gear storage. Most molded sheaths do provide grommeted holes or slots through which to attach your own pouches, although some creativity might be required. I've had good luck tying on nylon folding knife sheaths and GI compass pouches with a two-piece soap dish inside; a couple of times I've sewn my own from seat-belt strapping.

All of my own survival knife kits start with the compact Blast Match fire starter and a good liquid-filled pocket compass tied by its neck lanyard to the sheath. Each of them also carries a Maglite AAA Solitaire flashlight tied to the sheath by 2 feet of cord that wraps around its body and stuffs inside. If these items are duplicated in a larger survival kit, that's okay, because each is lightweight enough and more than important enough to have a spare.

POCKET

I carry a pocket survival kit with me almost everywhere I go, even when I'm not in the woods. It usually resides in the breast pocket of my shirt or jacket, where it remains relatively unnoticed until needed—just as it was intended.

Prerequisite survival tools for this kit are the Basic Three: a good knife, an all-weather fire starter, and a compass to keep you traveling in a desired direction (see chapter 1). But in this instance the knife is carried inside the kit, which demands that it be a folder. To these I add a roll of 1-inch-wide safety tape to cover most medical needs, an AAA Solitaire flashlight, a spare battery, an eyeglass-repair kit, a Star Flash floating Lexan signal mirror, and any other necessities that fit the container and the situation.

My preferred pocket survival kit is carried inside a two-piece plastic soap dish ($1 at most drugstores) to contain smaller items that might otherwise fall out and to provide them protection from the elements. The packed soap dish is then slid into a GI compass pouch (about $3 at army-navy stores), which almost seems made to accommodate this container. A military ALICE (all-purpose individual carrying equipment) clip, also available at army-navy stores (about 75 cents), can be attached to the compass pouch, allowing the kit to be carried on the belt or clipped to a backpack strap.

DAY PACK

Like a full-size, fully equipped backpack, a day pack should be an entire survival kit in itself, capable of keeping its owner alive indefinitely under any conditions, only with fewer comforts. Some have disparaged the 15 pounds of gear I carry on my back whenever I'm away from camp, but only until someone slips with a knife, steps into a yellow jacket nest, runs out of drinking water, or gets devoured by blackflies.

Decent inexpensive day packs retail at department stores for under $15, but I prefer the heavier zippers and stouter construction of name-brand day packs such as the Jansport Air Wave ($70) or the Eagle Creek Sirdar ($90). Shoulder straps have to be padded and comfortable enough for all-day wear, and there should be several pockets and compartments that can be turned into dedicated first-aid, fire-starting, and other kits.

Inside the day pack I like to further segregate items into individual packages. Zipper-lock plastic bags have been a permanent part of my survival kit for decades, although those in my packs are usually laminated with clear plastic contact paper or strips of boxing tape to make them more puncture resistant. Eagle Creek also offers a fairly addicting line of zippered see-through watertight pouches covered with nylon mesh to add toughness. Called Pack-It Sacs, the smallest measures 7 ½ by 3 ½ inches and retails for $6.50; the largest is 14 by 10 inches and sells for $10.

Rolled inside a bivy, stuff-sacked, and shoved into the bottom of my day pack is an ultralight sleeping bag—I prefer Slumberjack's 20-degree Everest Elite ($120) to cover warmth and shelter in all types of weather. A Seychelle squeeze-bottle water filter ($35) or small day pack filter like the SweetWater WalkAbout ensure that any water found can be made safe to drink. A GI canteen, cup, and cover outfit makes boiling and cooking possible, and an ordinary tablespoon adds all the eating utensils a woodsman needs. It isn't the ideal choice for camping in comfort, but a well-equipped day pack can virtually guarantee its wearer's survival anywhere on earth.

BACKPACK

This is the survival kit so many folks were discussing prior to the Y2K computer bug, usually under the monicker *bugout pack.* Fortunately, the millennium bug wasn't the problem some had predicted, but large numbers of people now have a pretty good handle on addressing their most basic needs—food, water, warmth, and shelter—because of the experience.

Backpackers have it all covered. A typical man's pack will weigh about 60 pounds, or one-third of its bearer's body weight, which my own observations have shown can be carried more or less comfortably for about 10 miles per day by an average guy. Women should also abide by this rule of thumb, perhaps with special emphasis on gear made for ultralight backpacking.

Any full-size survival backpack should provide its wearer with at least five days' worth of food, based on an average daily consumption of about 3,500 calories. A mediocre woodsman dropped with an outfitted backpack into virtually any environment on earth can easily survive until his food stores are exhausted. And after the food is gone, a backpack can continue to provide for most of its owner's needs in relative comfort for an indefinite period.

Suitable backpacks will have lots of pockets in which to segregate individual kits. I prefer an internal-frame type backpack such as the Peak 1 Conquer ($130) for its narrower profile, which allows me to squeeze between trees and stay close to a rock wall on narrow ledges. External-frame backpacks, like Kelty's field-proven Super Tioga ($180) or the equally famous but less comfortable GI ALICE pack ($75), are better suited to carrying tie-on tools such as shovels and axes.

Being larger, a backpack can accommodate many niceties that can't be fitted into or onto a day pack. A full-size two-person tent, such as the Moss Starlet ($350), makes spending several days in one spot more tolerable, especially in foul weather. A closed-cell foam sleeping pad provides insulation from the cold ground when seated or sleeping; I especially prefer the Link Rest ($12) from Cascade Designs because two or more can be fitted together with their mortised edges to form a larger pad.

AUTO

Most motorists carry emergency items in the vehicles they drive, usually beginning with a spare tire and jumper cables, because flat tires and dead batteries are fairly common problems. But loading a car or truck for survival should entail a bit more planning than simply tossing a few things inside.

First, identify the dangers you are most likely to encounter. When I'm truck-camping off remote and rugged logging roads, I've learned to carry a large Corona Razor-Tooth handsaw ($25) like those used by tree pruners, because more than once a thunderstorm has toppled trees across the path leading out. A sturdy pointed shovel is an absolute necessity for clearing away mud from a hung-up frame, and I also carry a heavy-headed roofer's hatchet for chopping the occasional protruding stump from under the skidplates.

In a winter environment it makes good sense to have the clothing, blankets, and other emergency items you'll need to survive being stuck in a snowdrift for a prolonged period. In the winter of 1986–1987 a quartet of teenage girls endured being stuck for four days on a seasonal road near Traverse City, Michigan, a fairly well-populated area. None was dressed or prepared for a long walk through deep snow, and when their 4x4 Blazer ran aground on a snowdrift in open country, they were forced to sit there until someone eventually spied the roof of the dark-colored vehicle and came to investigate. Their only nutrition during the ordeal consisted of a roll of breath mints, but despite their suffering these girls were lucky.

One survival item I very much recommend for every vehicle in snow country is a pair (or more) of snowshoes. In the winter of 1997–1998, 100 people died in their cars on Interstates 70 and 80 when a powerful snowstorm swept across Illinois, Indiana, and Ohio. With all lanes blocked, snowplows were of no use, and rescue attempts by snowmobile proved futile in the deep powder. Even an inexpensive pair of working snowshoes in the 9- by 30-inch range would have been sufficient to carry nearly all of the victims to warmth and safety—which was seldom more than a mile away.

Another winter survival item I wouldn't be without in a car or truck is a long-handled square-nose grain shovel. A vehicle becomes stuck because the friction against its underside exceeds the amount of friction applied by drive tires against the underlying snow. In other words, the car's weight is lifted off its tires. Getting unstuck is seldom more serious than using a long shovel to clear away packed snow from the undercarriage, thereby replacing weight onto the tires.

In desert country a 5-gallon jerry can of drinking water is never a bad idea. Even in the Great Lake State I keep at least a gallon of potable water in my vehicle at all times as defense against the odd radiator leak or being stuck far from a water source. I also like the security of having a backpack water filter in my car's survival kit, because it allows me to draw engine coolant, fluid for windshield washers, or drinking water from virtually any ditch.

Tire-repair kits have been a part of my vehicular survival outfit for many years. While it is possible to puncture a sidewall on remote two-tracks, nearly every flat tire got that way because a nail, sharp rock, or other hard foreign object was pushed through a tire's tread under a vehicle's own weight. Inserting a tire plug or two, per instructions on the repair kit's package, then reinflating to 35 psi with a standard bicycle pump is generally much simpler than trying to jack up a 2-ton truck on soft ground.

Also, many new trucks are sold with a "doughnut" temporary spare tire unless a buyer notices and demands otherwise. A doughnut spare cannot be used on a 4×4 in rough terrain because of its different size and traction characteristics, which forces the drivetrain to work harder on that side and can damage the transfer case. Consider a proper spare tire to be valuable survival equipment when you're relying on a vehicle to get you into and out of remote country (I carry two).

Again, you won't want to simply toss these and whatever other survival items might be needed into your car trunk or pickup box. Like backpacks and day packs, vehicular survival items need to be segregated into dedicated kits that are as readily available or transportatable as they'll likely need to be.

For car or truck, too many unpleasant experiences have taught me to keep a large and comprehensive first-aid kit in a shoulder bag, where it can be snatched up and carried at a run. A plastic 5-gallon bucket with lid makes a durable, weathertight container for isolating and protecting most of the smaller survival kits.

SNOWMOBILE

I almost had to force a shoulder-bag survival kit onto the young couple who had dropped by to share their excitement about going on a four-day guided snowmobile safari into Upper Michigan's Huron Mountains. I shared their happiness because I've had the pleasure of roaming that large and still very wild region, but because of my experiences there I insisted that my friends take along a kit of basic survival tools.

As fate would have it, they needed the kit. The husband grudgingly strapped it across the back of his machine, where it bounced forgotten throughout 100-mile days. On the third day the couple dropped behind their group to answer a call of nature, thinking they could catch up easily enough by following the safari's trail. To their chagrin, well-used snowmobile trails branched in all directions (as I knew they would), and only the compass and map in their kit made it possible for them to choose the correct path from the maze before nightfall.

Snowmobilers frequently get into trouble because potential dangers are rarely part of the sales pitch employed by dealers who sell snow machines and accessories. Little or no mention is made of throwing a track, blowing a piston, or other mechanical failures, even though such breakdowns have been occurring since there have been snowmobiles.

More than a few snowmobile drivers—myself among them— have learned that packed snowmobile trails often will not support the weight of a walking person. Commonly, the crusted upper surface will support just enough weight to force a walker to bear down with his forward foot, then send him crashing knee deep with a bone-jarring thud. No one travels far under these conditions without snowshoes, which I believe are as essential to safe snowmobiling as a spare tire is to safe motoring.

RECOMMENDED SURVIVAL KITS

There are presently hundreds of manufacturers making thousands of items and different versions of the same item for the outdoor market. Several products are recommended by name in this book because they've performed well under conditions that have on occasion destroyed lesser counterparts.

But none of the recommendations made here can be written in stone. In three decades my own backpack and survival gear has evolved enough to convince me that many of the products I recommend here will be improved, replaced, or made obsolete in coming years. The basic needs—water, food, warmth, and shelter—will always be fundamental to survival, but today's survivalist is armed with numerous potentially lifesaving tools that were the stuff of science fiction only a few decades ago. Just the average outdoorsman of today is equipped to survive environmental conditions that were often fatal to previous generations, so are tomorrow's wilderness adventurers sure to be packing survival tools that haven't been invented yet.

With this caveat in mind, I offer the following roster of survival kits from my own collection. Each carries the essentials for staying alive under almost any conditions, but all can be augmented or changed as needed to better suit specific environments.

Knife:

> 1 Schrade Extreme survival knife
>
> 1 Blast Match fire starter carried in sheath pouch
>
> 1 Brunton Tag-A-Long pocket compass on lanyard
>
> 1 Maglite one-AAA Solitaire flashlight on lanyard

Pocket (includes survival knife kit above):

> 1 two-piece plasic soap dish to contain survival items
>
> 1 GI compass pouch to hold packed soap dish
>
> 1 ALICE clip for attaching kit to belt or straps
>
> 1 Brunton Tag-A-Long pocket compass
>
> 1 Blast Match fire starter

1 foil-laminated Mylar Space Blanket

1 Maglite Solitaire one-AAA flashlight

1 Star Flash signal mirror from Survival, Inc.

Day pack (including all of the above items):

1 Jansport Air Wave day pack with waist belt

1 Suunto GPS Plotter Compass

1 SweetWater WalkAbout water filter

1 two-D-cell Maglite flashlight

1 Integral Designs Sola tube bivy

1 GI-style plastic canteen with steel cup and case

1 200-weight polypropylene fleece sleeping-bag liner

1 first-aid kit:

   1 8- by 10-inch Eagle Creek Pack-It Sac to hold first-aid items

   1 roll ½-inch-wide safety tape for bandaging cuts

   1 small tube Neosporin or equivalent

   1 motel-size soap bar in zipper-lock bag

   1 dozen Steri-Strip butterfly sutures

   1 small roll gauze bandaging

   1 dozen aspirin (blood thinner, heart attack aid)

   1 dozen ibuprofen or acetaminophen tablets

   1 dozen electrolyte-replacement tablets

   6 individually packaged Benadryl capsules

   6 loperamide HCl antidiarrheal caplets

   50 multivitamin tablets (your choice)

   1 dozen hard candies (for hypoglycemia)

   2 air-activated heat packs (for treating shock)

1 dozen moleskin blister patches

1 dozen sewing needles, various sizes (splinters, etc.)

2 feet latex surgical tubing (tourniquets, slingshots)

1 plastic-laminated area map covering route

1 ultralight tarpaulin or Space Blanket

1 two-D-cell Maglite flashlight

8 granola or fruit-cereal bars

50 feet 550-pound-test parachute cord

1 tube-type mosquito head net (also prevents snow blindness)

1 roll toilet paper, flattened, in zipper-lock bag

Backpack (including all of the above items):

1 Eagle Creek Endless Journey backpack (detachable day pack)

1 Brunton 8099 Eclipse compass

1 Peak 1 Crestone 15-degree mummy bag (replaces liner)

1 Slumberjack Predator bivy (replaces tube bivy)

1 PUR Scout water filter (replaces WalkAbout)

1 fishing kit:

> 10 fishhooks, long shank, various sizes
>
> 20 split-shot sinkers, various sizes
>
> 1 spool 20-pound-test monofilament fishing line

1 Swiss Army–type mess kit with pot, nested dish, cover

6 envelopes ramen noodle soup in large zipper-lock bag

4 packages dehydrated potatoes, repacked in zipper-lock bags

1 Marlin Model 25 .22-caliber bolt-action rifle

2 50-round boxes Yellow Jacket .22 Long Rifle ammunition

Automobile:

> 1 day-pack survival kit
>
> 1 radial tire plug kit
>
> 1 standard bicycle pump
>
> 1 tire-pressure gauge
>
> 4 road flares
>
> 1 gallon drinking water (5 gallons in desert country)
>
> 5 gallons gasoline in jerry can (about 100 miles' worth)
>
> 1 four-D-cell Maglite flashlight
>
> 100 feet ½-inch nylon rope
>
> 1 approximately 10- by 10-foot vinyl tarpaulin
>
> 1 long-handled shovel (pointed type in summer, flat in winter)
>
> 1 pair snowshoes rated to carry 250 pounds (winter only)

Snowmobile:

> 1 day-pack survival kit
>
> 1 pair Atlas Model 1033 9- by 29-inch snowshoes (no smaller)

Index

folding, 77-79
sharpening, 92-95, *93, 95*
varieties of, 110
knots, *87-91,* 87-92

lakeshores, 10
landmarks, 9, 10, 11, 80
   absence of, 14
   map compasses and, 12
   vectoring and, 197
lean-to shelters, 42-44, *43*
lichens, as tinder, 30
Link Rest tent, 113
Little Dipper (Ursa Minor) constellation, 22, 23,
   24, 25, 27
Lyme disease, 101

machetes, 47, 78
magnetic north pole, 8, 14
maps, 11, 79-81
   magnetic declination and, *14,* 14-15
   topographic, 15-19
marshes, 15
medical treatment, 68-70
   first-aid kits, 73, 74
   medicines, 71-73
   for skin lacerations, 70-71
   vitamin tablets, 73-74
minerals, 59